ISP SECURITY WARRIOR TRAINING

Dedicated to all those fighting to preserve Western values.

ISRAELI
SECURITY
WARRIOR
TRAINING

Garret Machine

Paladin Press • Boulder, Colorado

Also by Garret Machine:
Combat First Aid: A Citizen's Guide to Treating Battlefield Injury (video)

Israeli Security Warrior Training
by Garret Machine

Copyright © 2011 by Garret Machine

ISBN 13: 978-1-61004-180-5
Printed in the United States of America

Published by Paladin Press, a division of
Paladin Enterprises, Inc.,
P.O. Box 1307
Boulder, Colorado 80306 USA
+1.303.443.7250

Direct inquiries and/or orders to the above address.

Visit our website at www.paladin-press.com.

CONTENTS

INTRODUCTION

This book contains concepts and techniques I learned while in the Israel Defense Forces (IDF) and later while serving as a bodyguard for the Israeli Ministry of Defense. Israel has a slightly different way of dealing with matters of security. It has each element compartmentalized and specialized; yet at the same time, it creates a synergy between the different professions within security to achieve cohesiveness. Israel does not want a security warrior who is good at everything; it wants one who is a master at his field of expertise and responsibility.

For instance, in the U.S. Secret Service, agents spend years investigating financial crimes and counterfeiting before transitioning to actual bodyguard work. In Israel, it is all about the development of the security warrior mindset. Israeli security warriors must first serve a minimum of three years in combat as an officer with a combat infantry unit or elite outfit. Then after a careful selection process, they are chosen for training on specific security protocols, procedures, and combat doctrine for their specific detail. Again, this is in pursuit of developing a purpose-built security-minded warrior.

My first experience with security and bodyguard duties in Israel was when I was still a soldier in the IDF. I was serving as a combat soldier in the Duvdevan Unit, which specializes in urban warfare, low-intensity conflict, counterterrorism, and hostage rescue. One of our mandates was serving as the premier counterterror unit in the West Bank and Palestinian-controlled territories. It was the first quarter of 2008, January if I remember correctly, and then U.S. President George W. Bush had come to Israel. Bush and his convoy were scheduled to make their way through the West Bank and visit the capital of the Fata-controlled Palestinian authority, Ramallah, and then on to Bethlehem. When his trip was announced the week before, there was a lot of civil unrest among the Palestinians and terror factions. The protestors burned U.S. flags and threatened President Bush if he came to Ramallah. These were serious threats, and there was a lot of tension in Israel about the impending trip.

My unit was tasked with protecting President Bush on this portion of his trip. We were to liaison with U.S. Secret Service agents and act as a reaction team for any serious terror threat that materialized. We staged in an area just outside and along his intended route and waited. From about seven in the morning until the afternoon, we hid in the shadows and held that position for hours, waiting relentlessly just in case. If his convoy were to be attacked or any other organized violence broke out against him, we were there to react. In the end nothing happened, but I did spend a lot of time with the U.S. Secret Service agents, which allowed me to learn about the job I would find myself doing a few months later for the State of Israel. The same job, yet executed differently.

Israeli Security Warrior Training was designed as a guide for various urban, tactical, and security operations, as well as building, managing, equipping, and training a security team. It is not an absolute guide on the subject of security—it won't teach you everything there is to know about security. Such a task would be impossible, as well as counterproductive. My intent is to teach you key skills that you can adapt to your specific assignments. This manual covers security for special-operations units tasked with security-type missions. The tactics, principles, and procedures aren't standardized training doctrine for any one unit in Israel, but general principles for all-around security work.

This is a manual and therefore technical in nature. I have done my best to make the concepts and instructions comprehensible to beginner and veteran security professionals alike. I organized the material into six parts to make it more accessible: fundamentals; security warrior training; skills; threat assessment and response; dealing with suspicious people, vehicles, and objects; and mobile security.

Finally, I would like to stress that the most important security concept in this manual is the development of the security warrior mindset. With that in mind, let's start with the security fundamentals.

PART ONE

FUNDAMENTALS

Part one of this manual defines what it is to be a security warrior and what being one entails. It outlines his duties to himself and his client, and the security principles and rules that govern how he does his job. Because equipment and communications are so critical to any security mission, it pays special attention to those basic needs. Finally, it shows how the security warrior puts all these into play as he prepares to face each new aspect of his security job.

CHAPTER 1

The Security Warrior

First, you are not a security guard or officer—you are a *security warrior.* This mentality needs to be adopted before you're put in a situation during which you're asked to risk your life in the performance of your duty. You must be ready and willing to counter violence and aggression with a greater level of violence and aggression. As a security warrior, your two main objectives are to prevent and to deter. High-intensity training is the only way to acquire the warrior mentality and achieve these objectives.

A warrior must be ready for any threat from any enemy at any time. To become a confident and effective security warrior, you must attain an exemplary level of proficiency in specific areas. Mastering hand-to-hand combat and physical fitness, searches and sweeps, pistol/rifle combat, tactical driving, security formations, force-on-force training, emergency medicine, and ongoing training in the field of security procedures and scenarios is crucial to your success and survival as a warrior. In the face of danger, you must be confident in *all* your skills—or you will succumb to the enemy.

Though security operations most often involve teams, you must be capable of functioning on your own as a lone wolf if required. The lone warrior concept is that you are the *only* solution to the problem. You must rely only on *your* knowledge and skills. Other team members may be helpful at times, assist you in your mission or acting as backup in an emergency. However, unlike when team tactics are being used, the lone warrior doesn't function as part of a larger tactical unit because of the reactionary nature of the job. Critical incident response means dominant threat neutralization. You can't delegate to anyone else the responsibility of solving a life-threatening situation. Your work is reactionary and defensive.

In this book I want to give you, the security warrior, the concepts and skill sets necessary to be confident enough to confront potentially dangerous security situations, whether you are part of a security team or forced to act alone. With this confidence, you will be able to take charge of the situation, the client, and yourself.

SECURITY WARRIOR VS. MILITARY SOLDIER

The second point to consider is that you are not a military soldier. When facing a terrorist threat, it is always more challenging for the security warrior to defeat the terrorist than it is for the combat soldier. This means that the security warrior's job is essentially more difficult than that of military personnel. A security warrior operates alone; this means that his initial reaction will be to that of surprise. He will have to react independently to immediately bring about a response that will lead to a solution.

This is different than the environment in which a team of 12 or more soldiers operates. Security team members are usually armed with handguns, while soldiers have access not only to pistols but also rifles, grenades, and other types of arms. The soldier works offensively, thereby increasing his chances of accomplishing his mission. The security warrior works defensively, giving him one chance to win or lose— to kill the terrorist or be killed by him. Failure will result in civilian loss of life, and possibly a great number of deaths. The security warrior is anticipating a surprise, while the soldier is delivering a surprise. Action will always beat reaction in terms of speed. This constant anticipation leads to complacency, the enemy of all security forces. An undercover security warrior carries about 17 rounds of pistol ammunition, whereas a soldier can have more than 180 rounds of rifle ammunition. More firepower means a greater chance of success.

There is no support staff waiting to assist security warriors in combat, whereas soldiers will have support from tanks, helicopters, and other units in the area as needed or dictated by the offensive plan. When a security warrior is alerted, he will have at most three critical minutes to solve the situation. When a soldier is in battle, he has spent several months preparing for this specific battle, and usually he dictates the length of time necessary to complete the mission. In other words, the combat mission of the soldier has a preplanned start, movement to contact period, enemy engagement, and extraction. In a crisis, a security warrior has no control over the time, location, or means of attack; he only has his skills. It is difficult to plan for the unknown and for circumstances that might be out of your control. On the other hand, a soldier usually enters a crisis with a mapped-out plan of how to conduct the mission to his best advantage.

This book will teach you the skill sets needed as a security warrior, when success or failure rests on you alone.

CHAPTER 2

Duties

Your duty as a security warrior is to protect life and property to the best of your ability. Even though it is impossible to create a situation of absolute security, you must try to achieve this goal. You must act as the barricade between the threat and the person or property you're guarding. Being a human barrier between the haves and have-nots is a lot to take on, which is why you must know the tactics involved in doing so. The most efficient way of fulfilling your duty to protect people and property can be broken down into four categories:

1. Containment
2. Prevention
3. Gathering of information
4. Reaction

Containment, by definition, is to be capable of holding something within. If a security warrior can't hold his guarded personnel or objects within a safe zone, he isn't doing his job. When a security warrior is told to contain a certain area, he is expected to enclose the facility or individual in a sterile area over which he has control. As the security in control of that area, you and your team must know everything about your mission. If you come across something unexpected or previously unknown to you, you must consider it dangerous until it can be thoroughly investigated. Once an area is deemed sterile, nothing or no one can enter or leave it without being authorized by you or your team. If you can contain the people you're protecting in a sterile area, then they will be out of harm's way.

A security warrior must be an intelligence-obtaining machine. With enough practice, you will be able to see everything in your environment and become aware of any possible threat in everyday life. This is a good way of training to function as a machine. With good intelligence, you have already won half the battle. If you don't have a plan based on solid intelligence, failure will be the ultimate result. To formulate a successful plan, you need to know everything: the primary and alternate travel routes, hospital locations, known threats in the area, possible points of weakness, and all other relevant information that would go into planning the specific details of your operation. From identified weak points and threats, you must think of all possible solutions and discuss them with the team. Being creative is seeing what others see but thinking something different. But your creativity alone can't match that of the group.

You need to do all that is possible to prevent a situation from escalating to the level of deadly force. If there is dangerous activity happening in the area where you're working, you must get the client away at the first sign of trouble. If there is a fight breaking out or criminal activity close to the client, move him away from the scene to prevent any accidental encounter with danger.

Aside from avoiding obvious danger, you should take certain precautions to avoid weakening your mobility and that of your client. For example, proper parking is essential to ensure access to immediate mobility if necessary. Parking properly consists of back-in parking instead of head-in parking, and the motor should be left running at all times if possible. Instead of parking in a parking spot where you could be boxed in, park where you know no one can block you in. If someone does block your vehicle, you will be forced to fight or flee, like a wild animal that is being cornered. You do not want this.

Duties

A security warrior must hone his reactions so that they are instinctive, when acting either alone or as part of a team. For example, consider the following scenario. John and Ben are on a bodyguard detail for the police chief, who is giving a speech to community leaders and press. Halfway through the speech, a man throws an egg, hitting the police chief directly in the face. Immediately Ben closes distance to the assailant and takes him to the floor, subduing him until he no longer resists. While Ben pursues the assailant, John moves the police chief out the back door. Ben handcuffs and removes the egg thrower, handing him over to the police for questioning.

In the above scenario, John and Ben exemplify a reactionary force action. Ben responded to the threat immediately with overwhelming violence and force. The continued use of force until the assailant no longer resisted was necessary not only to eliminate the immediate threat but also to intimidate spectators into keeping their distance (it may also deter them from pursuing future attacks). Once John realized that the egg-thrower was no longer a threat because of Ben's swift action, he ushered the police chief out the back door and into the escape vehicle. After initial contact with the enemy, there will be a lull in the combat or some other indicator of threat suppression. This is the

Two examples of how to restrain a suspect using cuffs: against a wall and on the ground.

13

indicator for the primary man to move the protected parties out and for the secondary force to hold the line or advance to facilitate their escape.

All the security basics were in play: the security warriors reacted quickly and decisively to contain the threat and remove the protected party from additional danger. Additionally, the escape vehicle was parked close by in a sterile, unblocked area, with the driver waiting in the running vehicle.

CHAPTER 3

Security Principles

An examination of the finer points of building a security system is necessary to fully understand the role of the security warrior. This book examines the primary security principles you'll need to do that. It contains numerous lists and rules that security personnel need to know. These lists are essential to putting together a security detail to guard an installation, an individual, or a group. Good security is all about following lists and specific protocols. The lists will vary according to your assignment, but there will be lists in every security job.

Security is about absolute certainty. You must check and double-check everything. A good security warrior thinks in a strategic and analytical fashion so that he can see things the way the enemy or attacker will. First he is a warrior; then he is a security warrior. First he learns combat—how to fight, how to be aggressive—and then he learns the security procedures. First he learns the concepts of warfare and how to fight to the death; then he learns how to apply them to security. To create this concept of security, everything is based on manpower, equipment, and rules.

A security organization has three primary functions: management, reaction, and prevention. A security group is organized to specialize in one of these three functions. Groups within the organization will specialize in these three functions.

MANAGEMENT

Management handles all the logistics, including scheduling shift time, training, intelligence, payment, and all other aspects not related to actual combat. The person in charge of management must also have the warrior mentality and experience, even though he may no longer be involved in the physical guarding aspects. It is his responsibility to ensure that logistical issues don't distract security warriors from their roles.

REACTION

All security work is reaction oriented. The kind of action taken in response to a situation is specific to what the security warrior feels is necessary. In this manual I hope to instill in the reader the proper reactions to the most common types of security situations.

Reaction work is essential to the security warrior because his entire job is based on reacting to a potential threat. Contrast this with the role of a military warrior who participates in missions where teamwork is essential for success. In security work, having the element of surprise isn't possible for the good guys. For every force working against the security warrior, he must react with twice the force to secure domination. He wins by responding to violence in a more efficient and tactical manner than does the enemy. Speed and accuracy are key to being more efficient than the force acting against him. This is because the enemy gets to choose when, how, and where the attack will occur.

As a security warrior, you must have the ability to determine proper reactions to likely scenarios. A reaction is deemed proper if it is fast, accurate, and asserted with the correct amount of aggression. When reacting to a critical incident, you have only that fleeting moment to determine the fate of your client, your teammates, and yourself. There is no going back and no changing your mind. Thus, you must know how you will react to every possible situation before being forced to do so in real time. You achieve this knowledge through proper training and mindset. When reacting to a dangerous situation, you must know that you are fighting to save lives. As a security warrior, you must begin every day with the confidence that you can fight for your life—and the lives of those whose safety and security are your responsibility—*and win.* You must be ready at all times to react and successfully destroy any threat. Only through aggression and superior violence will you be able to prevail in the mayhem that is a crucial part of your job.

PREVENTION

Prevention is the optimum solution for any security problem, as it is better to avert trouble than to have to react to it. It is always better to avoid a fight than to fight and win. Security personnel tasked with this prevention function are often called *checkers.*

Though not warriors themselves, checkers are critical to the mission because they can foresee trouble and prevent a situation from escalating to a full-blown assault. Checkers (who are usually female) must be experts at interviewing and searching, and must ask the right questions of any individual trying to enter a sterile facility. Their job is to assess whether this person is a threat and to determine his identity. Searching all persons (including any electronics, bags, packages, or other items they have on them) before allowing them to enter the facility is a crucial part of their job. Checkers know how to work with specialized equipment for searching people and their belongings for weapons, and can also identify false documentation. If there is any doubt whatsoever, checkers call the manager or a security warrior. Checkers can check people's IDs and belongings, and they can ask questions and be aggressive if necessary to pressure people into reacting on the spot. They can do this without hesitation because undercover warriors, who are watching closely nearby, will protect them while they do their jobs. If the checkers are threatened in any way, the warriors will be ready to ambush the potential threat with overwhelming speed and precision.

CHAPTER 4

Rules/Combat Procedures

The rules/combat procedures explored in this manual cover all the doctrines to tactical situations a security warrior may face. The system will always be greater than the warrior; thus it is your job to understand the system in which you will be operating. (By system I mean the rules, procedures, and protocols that govern your behavior.) By understanding the system, you will be able to maneuver your way through your current situation with skill and confidence. This confidence is necessary to dominate the terrorist. Once you understand the rules, you can work within the system in the most efficient manner.

These security rules contain vital information, such as justification for drawing a weapon and shooting someone. In a hostage situation, the rules will tell you the exact measures and procedures that should be taken. Having a concise set of rules allows all the warriors on the team to be on the same page so they can function as a cohesive unit.

The rules will dictate your firing orders with regard to the environment you're working in and the level of hostility you will face there. One region of the world may require more liberal firing orders than another region. However, there are general firing orders that, regardless of your location, must always be obeyed. These firing orders are there so that you can fall back on them if you're ever in doubt. No matter where the warrior travels, the general firing orders will remain true, whereas the variables specific to each region are subject to change. Variables include the laws of the nation you're working in, the political climate of the region, and known threats.

General firing orders dictate that there must be three elements present to draw a weapon on someone: means, motivation, and capability. *Means* includes the equipment or devices to do harm, such as a hand grenade or anything that can be construed as a weapon. *Motivation* is the will or declaration to use that means to harm a person—i.e., to kill or injure. Let's say you spot someone in your area of operation with a pistol under his jacket. This is an example of means, but not necessarily of motivation. He has a gun, but he isn't doing anything threatening or telegraphing his intentions of using the weapon. An example of motivation without means would be the declaration of a jihad against the West without the presence of weapons. If a person draws a weapon and declares death to the police commissioner under your protection, then you have evidence of both means and motivation. Finally, *capability* means the ability to act in that moment. A man with a knife is not currently capable of doing damage from 100 meters away. Capability is an important parameter when deciding whether to fight and defend the protected or to flee to safety.

Throughout this book you will find many rules and combat procedures, but below are some general ones. Some rules and protocols are specific to the organization, country, and current threat levels. Below I will list some general combat procedures, but remember that no question should go unanswered when it comes to life and death. By this I mean that you make sure you know everything you can about your mission, your client, your enemy, and your team.

- Know your firing orders for the specific mission and circumstances.
- When the gun comes out, you are either moving or shooting. Never both and never neither, until the threat is neutralized.
- Always know your designated and alternate travel routes. Memorize them and be able to switch at a moment's notice.

Rules/Combat Procedures

- Know your route's points of weakness, as well as your facility's points of weakness.
- Always vary your routes and routines.
- Never let the enemy out of your sight until he is no longer a threat.
- Check your gear before every shift, including your radio, weapons, vehicle, and so forth.
- Practice your combat skills and procedures regularly (a minimum of once per month): shooting, fighting, driving.
- Know your client and make sure he knows your combat procedures.
- Micromanage every detail.
- Check and double-check everything.
- Use lists and follow your combat protocols.
- Obey the local laws of the land.
- Always wear your seat belt.
- The overriding rule is that *end results count.* Break any rule and sacrifice everything to save human lives. That's what you do—everything else is just circumstance.

CHAPTER 5

Equipment/Technology

Security equipment includes all the materiel needed to make a successfully functioning security system. Each security detail and each installation to be defended will require specific equipment. The unique equipment should be purchased initially, and then it should be expanded/upgraded as technologies necessitate and budgets allow.

Security equipment includes everything from cameras and motion detectors to guns and gates. Again, as with all aspects of security, equipment needs are specific to the situation, but certain pieces of equipment are universal for security assignments. Chief among these is some type of device for communicating. The security manager needs to have radio capability so he can communicate with the warriors on site and so the warriors can report what they see back to headquarters. Another crucial piece of security equipment for many security missions is one or more cameras. Cameras should be in place so the manager can watch what the checkers are checking. The more eyes on the unknown public, the better. Metal detectors and ID scanners are useful in order for checkers to do their job properly. Checkers also need panic buttons to summon the security warriors when they sense possible danger.

Success in the security field depends very much on the quality of the equipment available to the security team. Manpower can only take you so far without having the proper equipment. After all, you don't bring a knife to a gunfight.

RECOMMENDED EQUIPMENT LIST

At all times, each security warrior should have the following basic combat equipment on his person:

- Primary weapon (pistol or rifle), cleaned and inspected
- Secondary weapon (pistol) if using two weapons
- One to three high-capacity magazines for pistol; six for a rifle
- Communications gear (radio/phone)
- Sport shoes for running, sprinting, kicking, climbing, and driving
- Pants with cargo pockets, but not camouflage
- Digital watch with timing function
- Identification and cash in the form of U.S. currency (recommended: $500)
- Concealable knife for utility and combat (nothing large)
- Trauma first aid kit (detailed in Chapter 10)
- Specialized equipment for specific missions (e.g., surveillance gear, night vision goggles, or explosives)

Equipment choices will vary based on the needs, procedures, and budget of the group. Ideally, the team will purchase the best equipment that money can buy, top-of-the-line gear. The gear must be durable, reliable, and simple to operate. All gear must be familiar to all team members, even if it is routinely used by only one or two staffers. Each man will have the exact same equipment and gear: same weapons, same caliber, same radios, and so on for all combat-related gear. This is because each man may be tasked with any role on the team at any given moment, or he may need to use another warrior's equipment in an emergency.

Durability is a key element when dealing with equipment, and this is especially so with electronics. I have found Motorola radios and Nokia cell phones to be the most durable and user friendly. Other high-technology equipment and touch screens should be avoided whenever possible. Stick to proven gear that will work for everyone and last a long time. Glock pistols and Colt M4 Commando rifles are among the best weapons out there for security work and urban warfare.

The warriors must check all the equipment—including weapons, optics, communication gear, and vehicles—before each outing or shift. Further, a specialist for that particular piece of equipment must examine it on a regular basis (e.g., monthly) to ensure that it is functioning properly: a mechanic for the trucks, an armorer for the weapons, and a technician for the radios.

CHAPTER 6

Communications

Throughout the day communication with the headquarters command is vital to provide concise situation briefings. Communication should be kept short: the objective is to convey needed information, not to engage in distracting conversation. The information conveyed needs to include specific details so that commanders can make decisions based on that information. Communication is directed to a war room or dispatch in the facility. This room contains phones, cameras, monitors, computers, managers, and dispatchers, and it controls *all* communication with outside entities, including police, fire, and rescue personnel.

Locations of actions and enemies, how many attackers are dead and how many still alive, and all other data should be disclosed in the first dialogue. If a warrior is engaging an enemy, then communication is done after the fighting is completed. Do *not* radio the situation in before responding to the threat. Engage and destroy, and then radio headquarters to request backup and report the situation. Use codes to communicate as much as you can to keep dialogue secret.

Codes need to be built into your combat doctrine, and each warrior must memorize them. This means that locations at or around your facility must be codified and memorized by all security staff. Further, situations and descriptions should also be memorized and their use and dissemination practiced among the teams and dispatch/war room control personnel. All communication goes through dispatch. This keeps things in order in a chaotic situation. A typical dialogue might sound like this: "Garret at train (location code name), 3 sammies (enemy code name) neutralized, vehicle suspicious egg, sammie suspicious egg (bomb code name for a car bomb and suicide belt)."

Dispatch can then take this short codex and issue precise directions based on the intelligence it imparts. They will first convey the information to the warriors closest to the location and situation and then your location and situation. Then the other warriors will come to help you if they can. Simultaneously, they will pan their cameras and listening devices to the "train" location to get a visual contact on the situation. They will record the events as they unfold for documentation, which will prove useful later as a learning aid. They will use a single-word code to alert the other warriors that a lockdown and an "under attack protocol" must be put into play. They can then contact the police bomb squad, paramedics, and fire department.

When in the field or out on assignment, it is best to have redundant communication systems (e.g., a radio system and a cell phone). Remember the old saw: two is one, and one is none.

CHAPTER 7

Shift Preparation

Each shift will have unique problems, challenges, and characteristics, so it should start with a meeting to prepare all the warriors and checkers for their day and their mission. Before assuming positions, the team members meet with the team leader or manager. At this meeting, the leader discusses any special circumstances or new intelligence dangers specific to the shift, such as visiting VIPs, new threats intercepted or received, or natural disasters or political unrest that might result in evacuation. The team leader then asks each team member if there are special circumstances that might affect his performance. For example, a sprained ankle would likely prevent a member from sprinting, or an upset stomach might distract a checker from needed details. The morning briefing is also a good time for mini-training sessions and refreshers. For example, you might randomly ask: "What would you do if . . ." or "What is the best route to the closest trauma center from . . .?" Or you might direct a checker to search a person with a hidden weapon.

When the new team reports in to relieve the retiring one, its members need to do an equipment check, using a checklist, to ensure that all gear is present and in working order: radios, guns, cuffs, and a full vehicle check. Next they need to do a preliminary search of their area for bombs and suspicious persons before taking their positions. Then at random intervals during the shift, each warrior should conduct a brief search or mini-patrol in his section to make sure that no new dangers are present. The number and scope of these patrols or searches should be predetermined, based on exposure and shift time, and the operatives should strictly adhere to them.

Each warrior must be "cocked and locked," ready to destroy if necessary. A checker must be alert, sharp, and focused for the day's work of interviewing, checking IDs, and searching belongings. Following these set procedures for shift preparation helps to ensure this readiness.

PART TWO

SECURITY WARRIOR TRAINING

Training is the second-most important element in security operations, next to experience. But you need the right training to gain the experience to do the job. That's what this section is designed to do: outline the various training programs you must master before you can become a security warrior. The best security warrior training programs follow a linear outline conducted over a three-month course: five days a week with 12-hour days. Segments include physical fitness, combat shooting, trauma first aid, tactical driving, and academic courses on protocols and procedures.

Just as important as *what* is taught in the training courses is *how* it is taught. The courses should be fun, interesting, and challenging. Most important, they should be high intensity so that each trainee is conditioned to the point of becoming a programmed robot that can react quickly, smoothly, and efficiently to a given situation according to strict procedures and tactics. The goal is to turn each man into a warrior-machine when he performs his duties.

Finally, just going through a training course isn't enough. This section will show how to test your new skills to see if they measure up to those of a security warrior. **NOTE:** This manual is *not* intended as a substitute for professional security training, nor for specialized training in any of the specialties mentioned. Qualified instruction in each is essential to your success as a security warrior.

CHAPTER 8

Physical Fitness

A warrior must be strong and fit. So, a security warrior training course must include physical fitness, designed around a daily hand-to-hand combat segment. The fitness component should last about one hour a day, with an additional Krav Maga or hand-to-hand instruction of about two hours a day for the entire course. The hand-to-hand training should focus on aggression training and basic combat skills. This is in addition to daily tactical-shooting scenarios, technical shooting, and classroom sessions.

After the initial training course, fitness training will be your responsibility, and it should be conducted on a regular basis. A fitness-training log monitored by the team commander will help you maintain this regimen. Every six months a fitness test should be administered as a stand-alone session.

HAND-TO-HAND COMBAT

In general, hand-to-hand combat needs to be done after shooting training. A fine motor skill should come before a gross motor skill to maximize the effectiveness of both training sessions. As a security warrior, you must be fit and well versed in unarmed combat against a gun, knife, stick, and multiple unarmed attackers. You don't need to be a mixed martial arts fighter, but you must have some basic skills and, more important, be trained to be aggressive. You will be fighting to save lives (yours and those of your clients and teammates), not for a trophy. The objective of the combat won't be focused on points or a tap-out, but rather on escaping quickly without being pursued.

A basic principle of security work is that you must always respond to threats and aggression with greater aggression. With this mentality and a solid skill set, you will have confidence in dealing with violent encounters at close range when employing a gun is slower than using the hands, such as during a knife attack. You must also develop an all-or-nothing mentality on the force continuum. Forget fancy wristlocks and stun guns; in reality, when dealing with a serious threat (such as terrorism), you must be quick and devastating.

Here is a list of the skills the security warrior must master in hand-to-hand training:

- Basic fighting stance to maximize the effectiveness of weapons (hands and feet).
- Straight, hook, and uppercut punches; you must be able to

This aggression-training drill is designed to prepare security warriors to meet aggression head-on in real-life situations, such as the crowd-pass demonstrated here.

fire these off effortlessly in smooth, flowing combinations with speed.

- Front kicks to the chest and round kicks to the legs designed as the first blow before punching range. Stomp/blast kicks to fend off knives.
- Knee and elbow strikes for close-range and finishing blows.
- Knife defense from above, straight thrusts, and below and behind stabs. The technique must be simple: to disable, destroy, and create distance to draw.
- Stick defenses.
- Gun disarms from various positions.
- Suicide-bomber takedowns.
- Active-shooter takedown while he is shooting.
- Measures to keep someone from drawing a weapon.
- Weapon retention against someone who attempts to grab a gun from the holster.
- Arrest and takedown techniques.
- How to search and cuff a suspicious party.
- Weapon searches of people.
- Full-contact fighting, one-on-one in an organized class under expert instruction. Fighting against multiple attackers is also important. The fights should be fast (no longer than three minutes) and aggressive yet technical.
- Aggression drills designed to bring the fighter to exhaustion and test his fighting spirit.

Seek Krav Maga training from an Israeli who served in an elite unit of the IDF, who was a Krav Maga instructor in the IDF, or who was an Israeli Ministry of Defense warrior. The standards of Krav Maga training for the basic infantry soldiers in the IDF are primarily focused on fighting with an empty rifle and countering knives, hatchets, and sticks with an M16. The typical Krav Maga you find outside Israel is watered down and commercialized.

Krav Maga, which means literally "contact fighting," was

designed in the IDF for counterterrorism and combat, not sport. There are no belts, no competitions, and no real rules. The philosophy of Krav Maga is aggression and fighting spirit above all else. Krav Maga has a solution for every unarmed encounter against an enemy in a combat environment. There is more than one solution for tactical scenarios in Krav Maga, but not many, and all fall back on the basics. There is no such thing as "developing" or "creating" new Krav Maga techniques. It is a legitimate technique only if it has been proven in the field by the Israeli security establishment.

The Krav Maga instructor will be legitimate if he has a strong foundation in Israeli combat shooting as well, since in the IDF combat shooting and contact fighting go together. Training follows a simple yet proven structure:

1. Learn the expected skill or movement mechanics.
2. Practice them until they can be done consistently, without thought.
3. Once consistency is attained, add intensity, which is the speed element.
4. Add pressure. Functioning under pressure is the highest level of proficiency.

A great way to test combat skills under pressure is by integrating all three warrior aspects into a singe short drill. For example: sprint up a flight of steps or do 15 burpees. Then immediately do a crowd-pass to get to a knife attacker. Next, come to a firing line and fix three jammed weapons and fire one bullet from each into a head target at 5 meters. Finally, pick up a rifle and hit various targets at prescribed ranges.

The purpose of the drill is to test your resolve through the amount of effort you put into the fitness part. You will be judged on your aggression in the crowd-pass, your Krav Maga skills in the takedown of the knife attacker, and your weapon manipulation skills when you are forced to work under the pressure of a timer, your exhaustion, and that of your peers.

It's not enough that you can shoot fast and accurately. So can many competitive shooters. What matters is whether you can do it all after extreme stress and still get the results.

MINIMUM LEVEL OF FITNESS

The standard fitness requirements for entry into a security-training program should meet at least minimum levels, as outlined below, and must be maintained throughout the training course, as well as throughout your career. There is no place in any serious professional security outfit for an out-of-shape security warrior. (This rule also goes for police and military warriors, as far as I am concerned.)

- Pull-ups: 20
- Dips: 30
- 2,000-meter run in under 8:00 minutes
- Double crunches (lift both your upper and lower body simultaneously), 70
- 400-meter sprint in less than 70 seconds

Fitness training requires running, including sprints, medium distance (5 kilometers maximum), step running with 9 liters of water on your back, and short (20-minute) soft-sand runs. Pull-ups, dips, and push-ups should also be incorporated into the daily regimen, along with daily abdominal workouts. In an ideal situation, the dips should be done on gymnastic rings for stability, and pull-ups should be done on a fingerboard for grip strength .

Weight training is also excellent, as we must be able to easily manipulate external objects equal to our own weight. Never focus on muscle isolation. Train the whole body at once with functional core movements. We must be agile, accurate, fast, and, at the same time, powerful forces.

Fitness training should not take up more than an hour each day, five days a week. Each warrior must continue training throughout his career to maintain proficiency levels.

CHAPTER 9

Combat Shooting

The combat-shooting program is designed to bring the student to the optimum level in the shortest amount of time, so it needs to be simple to use and easy to learn. The program should use a system that will enhance motor memory for optimal preparedness in an emergency. When learning urban-warfare techniques, you need a system that can work when you operate both alone and as part of a team, as both situations call for the same skills and principles. Most of all, as stressed earlier, you must learn to fight and win independent of anyone else if you want to be a security warrior.

In-service combat shooting training must be done on a regular (I recommend monthly) basis and include not only static technical shooting exercises, but also dynamic scenarios, incorporating paint rounds (such as Simunition or FX) and tactical scenarios. A shooting theater is also a great way to train. The trainee can hit the screen with live rounds, the projector screen can be replaced like a paper target, and the scenarios on the screen will mimic reality and track accuracy. These and other technologies should be employed to bring training as close to reality as possible, while maintaining safety.

Each day of shooting should be accompanied by two or three hours of Krav Maga training, which will elevate your fighting spirit, mindset, and self-confidence, both with and without weapons.

Ideally, this will be one full day each month (as outlined in the previous chapter on physical fitness) after the initial training course.

Training on primary weapons and tactical scenarios will take up most of the course time and will be conducted on the shooting range, first with dry-fire practice and then with live-fire technical shooting, combat shooting, and surprise shooting drills, working up to full-scale tactical scenarios. Below are some of the skills that must be included in the course.

• **Weapon familiarization and maintenance.** The first things that must be taught are how the weapon works and how to clean it, take it apart, inspect it, and reassemble it. The students must be familiar with the functioning and mechanical workings of their weapons. At this stage of training, it is important to teach a standard method for clearing their firearms safely. This is a procedure that everyone must do perfectly and in the same way. Set the standard and then move forward.

This instructor ensures that rifles are cleared before the drill begins. All trainees are on one line, facing the same way, clearing their weapons in unison for safety.

- **Physical stress and hardships.** Both should be incorporated into the training program. Remember, this is a course for the young and fit, so this should not be a problem. The trainees must master a simple yet effective method of rapidly drawing and firing their weapons under duress and shock. The draw technique is from concealment because this is how the security warrior will draw most of the time.

- **Speed.** Speed training needs to be hard and fast, yet specific and not counterintuitive. Drills for speed of weapon draw, presentation, and aiming are all important, but trigger pull and grip will have possibly the greatest effect on first-shot placement. Sight picture, acquisition, and weapon manipulation for fast fire at close range must become second nature.

- **Weapon draws.** Gunfights are rarely determined by the draw, so we must train specifically for making the decision when to draw and how to use the gun.

Firing an EOTech-equipped M4 rifle from a kneeling position behind cover.

- **Firing positions.** Multiple firing positions (standing, kneeling, prone, supine) must all be practiced as part of the regular training. Since about four hours a day will be spent doing dry practice, it is important to make the most of that time.

- **Stoppages.** A super simple system for correcting jams and getting a gun working again must become second nature to the trainees. The simplest way to do this is to *fix* what you see, not *define* it. This means three basic jam-correction techniques: one for closed jams, one for open jams, and one for magazine changes. Tactical or voluntary magazine changes do not require training because they are done by will, not force. The closed jam is corrected by the slap-rack technique; the open jam requires removing the magazine to fully rack and clear the chamber. A magazine change should flow smoothly. Remember, you will have to change a magazine (Jam 3) eventually. When it comes to a jam, don't think of the proper name and other BS semantics. Think "I need to make this work in pitch black, while exhausted, and my life depends on it." In that case, "double feed" and "stove pipe" are handled the same as any other open jam.

Keep your focus on your objective as you change the magazine.

Decision making under pressure is crucial for security warriors. For example, not all these targets have weapons, so you must decide which to shoot first.

- **Closing distance.** This is an overriding principle in Israeli counterterrorism. It must be done and at all costs. This will become even more complex when dealing with multiple targets and incorporating decision making into your scenario drills.

DRY-FIRE VS. LIVE-FIRE DRILLS

Never forget that the learning curve is in the dry practice, and the solidification is in the live fire. So first master all the dry skills through repetition and then with live fire. Do every live-fire drill at least twice: once to do it wrong and once to get it right. During live-fire training, safety must be a top priority.

In live-fire training, there are a few priorities that need to be assessed in each participant: fighting spirit, aggression, speed, accuracy, use of cover, combat priorities, weapon manipulation, and communication.

Each drill will train for and emphasize one of the above principles;

some shooting drills will incorporate several or all of them. For example, a drill might include firing from cover, changing magazines from cover, or firing at multiple targets at various distances.

Specific firing techniques for bodyguarding are essential but should not be introduced until the basics have become instinctual and can be employed by each trainee when under pressure. As General George Patton observed, "Pressure makes diamonds." Incorporating too much information too quickly will only make things worse. Only after the basics are mastered can specific requirements be taught. Just as with the role of motor memory in the previously outlined skills, firing techniques must also become instinctual. The only way to test this instinctual nature is while the shooter is under pressure.

Walking formations and team tactics will be the next phase of training. The course is, in essence, a combat course, so team combat drills against an enemy must be incorporated.

VEHICLE SHOOTING

Vehicles are a big part of urban life, and they are an important component of security work as well. This means that the security warrior needs to be able to fire from a car window while either in the driver's seat or as a passenger. Further, this is where antiambush training will come into play. Fighting your way out of a car that is under attack while protecting your principal is a function that each team member must be capable of executing at each vulnerable point of a journey by car and convoy. This type of training should build up from one- to two- to three-man teams and then to multi-car convoys.

STRUCTURE FIGHTING

Structure warfare is part of advanced training, but it cannot be overlooked here. Although most attacks on individuals under close protection happen on the outside, combat inside a building is also a possibility. The same principles will apply in any urban setting.

Practice clearing rooms alone and in teams of two, clearing stair-wells, and advancing through a large industrial or commercial complex, such as a hotel, casino, amusement park, or other public venue where the team might find itself with the protected party.

SURPRISE AND HOSTAGE TARGET DRILLS

Surprise shooting drills are those where the target's location and situation are unknown to the security warriors. In these drills, the trainees will be confronted with hostage targets, shoot/don't shoot drills, and preloaded magazines with an unknown quantity of ammunition so they won't know when they'll have to change magazines. The instructor may have the students load for each other and hide shells in the stack to create jams for them to have to fix.

COMPLEX LIVE-FIRE DRILLS

All drills start with a physical stress, such as 30 seconds of punching a bag and sprints or burpees.

- Set up a shooting obstacle course with a 7-meter straight shot, a window shot at 5 meters, a shot fired from cover left at 3 meters, a shot fired from over a trash can or car hood at 10 meters, and a shot fired at a balloon at 10 meters from cover right. Students go one at a time with the instructor, and each target gets three shots, all sprinting of course, with 10 meters between each station. A magazine change is necessary. All movement is forward *and* lateral, not lateral only. Remember, the overriding principle of closing distance on the enemy is to overwhelm and neutralize him.

- Starting with a holstered gun, shoot at the hostage target at 10 meters; sprint 5 meters to cover left to fire at a 12-meter target; sprint 10 meters to cover right to fire at three targets at 7 meters.

- Sprint 75 meters to a torso target at 15 meters and fire three shots; then close distance to left cover and take on two targets and one hostage target. Sprint 20 meters to four targets: 5-meter, 7-meter, 12-meter, and 15-meter. Fire three shots at each target, performing magazine changes and jam corrections as needed.

- As a rule, when closing distance to a confirmed target, you must visually check all dead space (corner or crowd) if it is beyond arm's length on the way to the target or the next cover. If the space is within arm's length, check with an actual physical weapon point from cover. The check, which must be quick, is to confirm the safety of movement. Your inspection should also include open areas above and balconies behind you.

NOTE: For these exercises, students don't load their own magazines. The total number of rounds in each magazine is documented per event but is unknown to the shooters.

- Hit a punching bag for 30 seconds; draw and fire five shots on a target; sprint 10 meters to a hostage target and fire three shots; sprint 10 meters to a window target at 7 meters and fire three shots and then to a 20-meter target and fire three shots; close in 12 meters to a moving target and fire three shots.

- From inside a car: the driver pulls up, and the passenger shoots from the passenger side (defensively three shots) and then exits and sprints to fire on a 5-meter target in a crowd of targets; then he moves through the crowd to right cover and fires three shots. Next, he changes the magazine and fires one more round. He then sprints to a left cover target and fires three shots on a target at 5 meters.

- Starting with the gun in hand, the trainee moves to contact slowly to a doorway. He then opens the doorway and takes on three terrorist targets—one at center, one at extreme right, and one at extreme left—with good targets scattered about the room. Next he enters the room and moves to a hallway to fire on one target at the end of the hall. Finally, he closes distance to exit the hall into an open field and the target at 15 meters. All targets get five shots.

- It is the instructor's decision whether to perform two sets or more of the following drill. Create a drill on the spot with good and bad targets and hostage targets (as have been used for all drills). The drill should require a closing distance of at least 50 meters overall and two magazine changes. All shots are fired from behind cover.

- Final live-fire drill, with gun holstered under cover: the trainee hits the punching bag for 30 seconds and then draws his weapon and fires three shots on a target at 20 meters. He closes the distance in a straight line 10 meters to a wall and fires on the same target before opening the corner to find one bad guy in a sea of good targets. He closes the distance to the next wall (5 meters) to find the hostage target and fires three shots. Then he moves to the final cover to shoot at three static targets and one moving target. This drill requires two magazine changes, but the student doesn't know how many bullets are in each magazine.

WORKING IN PAIRS/TEAMS IN AN URBAN SETTING

Being able to work in pairs or teams is essential to the security warrior. You must have the ability to function as part of a small team for short periods in order to fight your way into or out a building for safety and security. This training also teaches team members that they can trust and depend on one another. Building the "I have your back and I know that you have mine" mentality, as well as being reassured that each team member has the capability to protect himself and you, builds trust from one warrior to the next. I cannot stress enough how essential it is to have this team trust. We train our men to

Firing from a door frame into a hallway and at the range.

A three-man team firing from cover.

operate as a tactical team of two, three, and four men. Training with more than four is not necessary.

Some of the basic skills the team members need to master are:

- Conducting two-, three-, and four-man room entries
- Clearing long hallways and corridors
- Clearing internal stairwells, door frames, or corners
- Defending or preventing vehicle ambush (three-man team)
- Executing cover-fire drills from a point of safety, such as a door frame

COVER FIRE SCENARIOS

- Two men firing into a room on opposite sides of the doorway
- Two men firing from the same side, from both kneeling and standing positions

Firing from cover with a handgun.

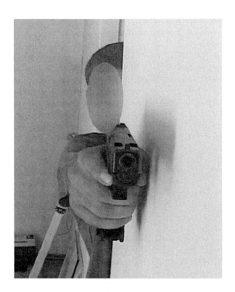

All you need are a barrel and an eye
when firing from around a corner.

- Carousel technique: one man fires from a door frame or corner while another joins him, from a kneeling position. A third man pulls out the standing shooter when he gets jammed, runs out of ammo, or is shot. The kneeling team member replaces the standing member, and the third teammate replaces the kneeling partner, while the first standing shooter repairs his weapon to get back into the fight. This process repeats for as long as is necessary or desirable.

There is no better way to test the focus and sharpness of the team members than making them do a live-fire team drill after physical exertion. Have them do sprints or burpees and then throw the team into a live-fire scenario. As always during a live-fire drill, safety is paramount.

RIFLE TRAINING

It is essential that a warrior be able to operate several weapons in an

Two men, one corner, one target . . .

emergency, including a handgun and a rifle. A security warrior must have access to a rifle at all times back at home base and while on the road. A rifle is critical when you are outgunned and outnumbered, and it also has excellent medium-range capability. I recommend a Colt M4 Commando with a Trijicon Reflex or ACOG sight, which is excellent for close-quarters battle as well as for ranges up to 200 meters in a bind.

The rifle is an easy weapon to master. In about two weeks of daily shooting, you can become quite proficient with it. As with any mechanical skill set, your rifle skills must be constantly refreshed and trained to maintain them at a desirable operational level.

COMBAT SCENARIOS FOR TRAINING

Practicing realistic combat scenarios is one of the most important areas of training. It is during these scenarios that the trainee learns and improves the most. Combat scenario training should be conducted on a monthly basis throughout the career of a security warrior.

Combat scenario training drills are tactical in nature and need to be organized as realistically as possible and executed with Simunition/FX–type rounds. Conduct these drills with predetermined scenarios and goals, and under the watchful eyes of several instructors. During the scenarios, each security warrior should role-play all the participants involved, including various types of enemies and members of the general public. All the training scenarios should be videotaped for review afterwards; in fact, you should videotape as much of your training as you can. Also there should be a debriefing after each scenario, emphasizing what was done well and areas that need improving. If you're in charge of the evaluation, use this order: something done well, something that needs improving, and something else done well. For example: "Good rate of fire; you need to work on the smoothness of your magazine changes; the aggression level was good."

With the rise of the communication age, the collective experience of security agents has been disseminated throughout the field. This is good because it gives you the opportunity to learn from a variety of different operatives. One term you hear a lot now in security chatter is *situational awareness*. The term is rather new to the industry, but the principle is ancient: being conscious of your surroundings at all times and using your experience and intuition to anticipate an attack and act preemptively. Scenario training is an invaluable tool for building situational awareness.

In training you are trying to build three essential facets of the warrior. The first is mindset, which is acquired through Krav Maga and other types of aggression training and the accompanying brain-washing. Next is the marksmanship necessary for firing at terrorists among civilians, which is acquired during the technical shooting portion. Finally, you want to be able to make tactical decisions. This ability (or lack thereof) will be evident in your decisions about where to move, how and where to fix a jam, and how to prioritize actions, among many choices you must make in the line of duty. Tactical scenario training builds and hones this ability to an expert level. Below are some generic scenarios, but you should customize them to fit your specific detail.

Scenario 1:

You're guarding the front gate of your facility, through which people enter to be checked, when a man from a far corner opens fire on people at the entrance. You draw your weapon and return fire as fast as possible while screaming for everyone to get down at once. This should put many actions into play: the checkers at the front alert the managers in the control room by radio to lock down the facility and call the police. While continuing to fire (shooting to kill) and scream at everyone to get down, you close distance with the attacker (while *not* being fired upon) as soon as possible, confirm the kill. Now look for any new threats, including those you told to get down. Search any suspicious people among the masses outside your facility. If you recognize any individuals as people who belong in the facility, or you need to protect them specifically, escort them in before you lock it down. Do a brief search of the area from which the enemy came. Search for unclaimed belongings or any suspicious objects, and then open a sterile area about 30 meters around the body of the terrorist you took down in case he is rigged with an explosive.

Return to the entrance and, with your gun in the strong hand and the radio in your weak hand, describe the situation and location as briefly and accurately as possible to the control room. Use a tactical location from which to do this. (A tactical location is one that offers a sight line to the threat, a clear fire line to the threat, ballistic protection from the threat, and a position from which you can defend and control your point of responsibility and respond to or reinforce other locations with ease.) If you're working undercover, display your identifying hat, vest, or other signal so that others responding to the situation can easily see and identify you. You don't take your eyes off the attacker, but you remain aware of the surrounding area and people. Lock in those people who are inside and disperse those outside. Lock down the facility until the bomb squad arrives to search the body and surroundings and clear the area.

Scenario 2

You're guarding the front gate when a man in a far corner opens fire on people entering the facility. As you engage this gunman, a second shooter opens fire from across the street. You fire three shots at each until one goes down. Then fight the other until both are down. Confirm neutralization on whoever is closer to you. Continue as in Scenario 1.

If one shooter runs after the other is shot, chase him with the intention of killing him. Remember, the checker at the front entrance must lock and secure the front door, and the whole facility remains on alert and in battle mode. Then search first for more human threats and then for object threats (that is, suspicious objects). When the bomb squad arrives on the scene, its members examine all unclaimed items.

Scenario 3

In a crowd outside your facility, a man starts to stab people in full public view. Whether he goes for the VIP or the people in the crowd, you use Krav Maga techniques because they may be faster than using your pistol at close range. Disable the attacker and stun him with overwhelming force and blows so you can draw your weapon and shoot to kill. Confirm the kill. Put everyone on the floor and move out as soon as possible.

Scenario 4

A man opens fire from around a corner from the facility at a distance of 70 meters and then runs away. You draw your weapon and escape with your VIP or lock down the facility instead of chasing the gunman. The great distance, the low likelihood of catching the terrorist, and the increased vulnerability for the VIP dictate that your priority is to escape to safety with the protected party.

Scenario 5

A strange man drops a backpack near your facility and then runs when you call out to him. You immediately open a sterile area around the object, lock down your facility, and call in the bomb squad from a safe distance behind cover.

PISTOL TRAINING QUALIFICATION

The following is an example of a pistol-qualification test for security warriors. To be used after the first week of training, this basic marksman's exam is based on the National Rifle Association's law enforcement instructor standards. Though not directly related to your field of tactics and combat, it still offers a good assessment of pistol marksmanship skills. To make it more applicable to the security warrior, you should draw from cover and after physical stress (such as sprinting or punching a bag).

- 15 meters/15 seconds: draw and fire three rounds, change magazine, fire three more rounds

- 7 meters/4 seconds: draw and fire three rounds to center-mass target
- 5 meters/2 seconds: from the ready with gun in hand, fire two rounds center mass
- 3 meters/2 seconds: draw and fire two rounds, one-handed

With the training program provided in this section, you can increase the realism of the training and the stress on trainees. At the end of the pistol-training section, a three-part exam should be given, which includes the following:

- A surprise-shooting drill with multiple targets, both good and bad, behind cover. It is a timed drill for speed and accuracy, including magazine changes and weapon transfers. Failure is shooting a hostage or good target. Fighting spirit and aggression are critical components of the trainee's grade. Only a combat veteran should judge such qualities.

- A timed technical-shooting drill with multiple targets at set distances, with magazine changes and various shooting positions (e.g., standing and kneeling). For example, here are two drills to practice.

7-7-7 pistol drill:
Start standing, facing away from the targets on the firing line with your weapon holstered. Sprint 25 meters away and then 25 meters back. A person will be standing on the firing line. You must move him aside, draw your weapon, and fire with one hand on a 8.5 x 11-inch sheet of paper as your first target. This target will be 7 meters away from you. Your weapon must be drawn from cover and will have either four, five, or six rounds in it. You are not meant to know exactly how many. After the weapon runs out of ammo, you change magazines and fire on a second 8.5 x 11-inch target. There must be movement during the magazine

change. The second magazine will also have four to six rounds in it. The second target will be 2 meters to the side and 1 meter to the rear of the first. You may use two hands after the magazine change. The total amount of ammo used in the drill will be 10 rounds. The total time it should take is seven seconds from drawing to firing the 10th bullet. Seven out of 10 rounds should hit the paper target. Ten hits in six seconds is possible.

This drill will test the warriors overall pistol combat capabilities for security work. The offset bullets in each magazine will prevent the men from counting, as there is no counting in combat. If the shooter fails to move during the magazine change or to engage both targets, the drill is void. Remember, you are either moving or shooting, never both and never nether.

15-7-7 rifle drill:
At 15 meters, repeat the same drill with the same configurations and parameters (except this time you use the M4 rifle and you are not drawing from cover). Fire 10 total rounds; there are either 4, 5, or 6 rounds in the first magazine. You move as you change magazines. From 15 meters away, fire 10 rounds at an 8 1/2 x 11-inch target. Your goal is to complete this in seven seconds with a seven-hit minimum.

- A shooting obstacle course that involves Krav Maga and shooting drills under extreme stress.

- An example might be running steps, passing a crowd, and then shooting multiple targets. Be creative and realistic. One of my favorite drills is to have one round in the gun, pass a crowed of eight, come to the firing line 7 meters from a hostage target, and fire. Use a shot timer and hit the head in under three seconds from draw time. For safety purposes, allow two seconds on the firing line before the go signal for situating yourself.

Another drill I like is the closing-distance drill. Start with 15 rounds in your weapon, standing at 25 meters from an 8.5 x 11-inch target. Draw from cover, shoot five rounds, close distance to 15 meters and shoot another five rounds, and close distance again on a sprint to 5 meters for a final five rounds. This drill can be done in under 18 seconds with 15 hits on paper.

CHAPTER 10

Trauma First Aid

Knowing how to administer first aid should be part of the security warrior's skill set. Not only is he a defender and taker of lives, but a security warrior is also a trained first responder. All members of the security staff need to be proficient in trauma first aid to be able to assist their clients, fellow warriors, and themselves if injured. This training is essential to preserve an injured person's life until he can be transported to the hospital or a paramedic arrives on the scene for further treatment. Security warriors are expected to be able to deal with trauma-related injuries, not medical-related problems, because of equipment and training issues and the nature of the work.

Every security warrior needs basic trauma first aid training. Ideally, a paramedic should conduct the course, and each individual should be trained and tested to meet the set standards of your organization and circumstances.

WHAT TO DO FIRST

The team should not focus on the treatment of injuries that aren't immediately life threatening. Resetting dislocated shoulders and setting and splinting fractures are all good skills to have but should not distract from eliminating the cause of such injuries. Your first

The proper way to load a fallen comrade for transport out of a danger zone.

medical priority is a life-threatening injury. The following material prioritizes the schematic of trauma first aid when you're under fire.

1. Return fire to neutralize the threat and maintain cover position. Destroy the source of the problem before fixing the damage done.
2. Move the injured man to a safe location out of the fire zone or behind cover for treatment.
3. Engage the safety on his and your weapons.
4. Task one or two men with helping the injured while the others stay engaged in the fight.
5. If the wounded individual is a member of your security detail, he returns to action after initial care is rendered (such as the application of a tourniquet), if able to do so.
6. The top priority is to stop arterial bleeding.
7. Next, secure the patient's airway.
8. If the patient is breathing, scan the body for more wounds.
9. If he isn't breathing, administer two rescue breaths and check his pulse. If there is no pulse, then there is nothing you can do in the

You must keep your weapon at the ready at all times, even when carrying a wounded person to safety,

field—call for help or transport immediately. If he has a pulse, continue with rescue breathing at one breath every five seconds while another man scans the body.

10. Do *not* perform cardiopulmonary resuscitation (CPR). There is no CPR in trauma. Your patient doesn't have a medical or heart condition—his problem is the direct result of trauma. CPR will cause more blood loss and break up any clots that have formed.

11. Scan the body for other injuries. Triage and address as needed, e.g., a sucking chest wound takes priority over a broken ankle.

12. Call for help or transport. Give the precise location of the injured party and a description of the enemies encountered. This is essential for the second wave of backup personnel arriving on scene to help. They must know who is good and who is at large.

13. If he is undercover, "sterilize" the wounded man for transport: remove weapons, communication devices, and any other sensitive identifiers.

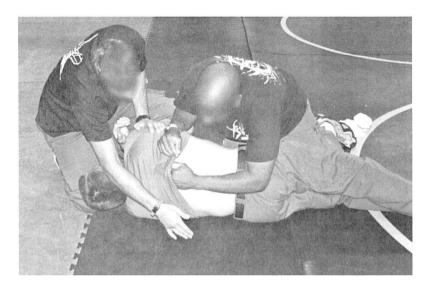

Scan the body for evidence of trauma.

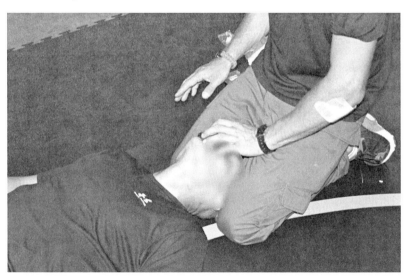

If there is reason to believe that a neck or back injury has occurred, then stabi-
lize the head and neck before transport if time and resources permit.

TECHNICAL SKILLS

Controlling Hemorrhaging

Excessive blood loss can lead to shock or the death of cells and eventually organs due to oxygen deprivation. As stated earlier, your first objective is to stop arterial bleeding—you can tell arterial blood by its bright-red color. (There are two other types of bleeding, venous and capillary, but they are slower and thus not as dangerous as arterial bleeding.) Because arterial bleeding is usually heavy due to its high pressure, it is hard to control, and you must act immediately. One can die in under three minutes from serious arterial blood loss. To stop the flow, go directly to the wound site and apply direct pressure, a pressure dressing, or a HemCon (no gloves yet). The likelihood of having gloves in the field and taking the time to put them on in such a situation is not realistic. Donning gloves is also unnecessary, as you should not have anyone on your team with blood-borne pathogens.

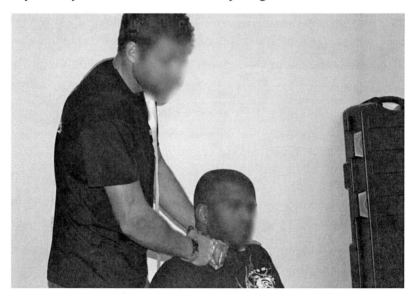

Apply direct pressure to the wound site to stop or control hemorrhaging. Use a HemCon and apply direct pressure for three minutes before tying it in place.

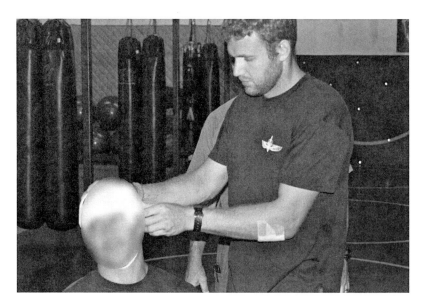

If direct pressure is not enough, you may have to apply a pressure dressing.

Remove the clothing around or covering the site, place the sterile side of the bandage directly on the wound, and tie tightly. Apply more pressure to stop bleeding if needed. You can apply a HemCon with an ACE bandage to hold it in place if needed. Place the white side over the wound with two minutes of pressure and then tie it in place. The pressure must be maintained until a medical professional takes over.

If the bleeding is from an extremity and you can safely do so, elevate the body part to slow the flow. **NOTE:** Do not elevate if a spinal or neck injury is suspected.

If the gauze or HemCon fails to stop the flow of blood and the patient is in imminent danger of dying, you should use a tourniquet.

Do not remove blood-soaked bandages because they may be helping with the clotting process. Generally a simple rule in trauma is to not remove what you place on an affected area.

How to apply the HemCon field dressing:

1. Open the HemCon package and remove it.
2. Cut the dressing to size it if necessary; the bandage must extend beyond the wound's edges.
3. Wipe away excess blood from the wound site, although some is necessary for the device to stick in place.
4. The dressing is sticky when wet so avoid water and other solutions.
5. Apply the dressing directly to the wound site or pack in the wound track.
6. Hold pressure until the bleeding stops, usually two minutes or longer.
7. Secure the dressing in place until it can be removed for end care at a medical facility.

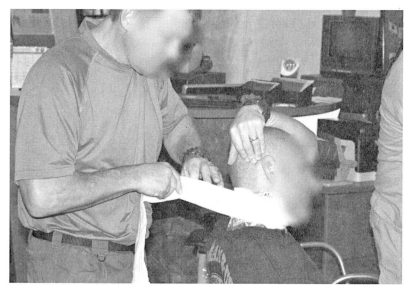

Securing a HemCon to the neck of an injured man. The HemCon can be cut, stuffed, and folded into the wound site. Wound packing is common but requires proper training.

Applying a Tourniquet

A tourniquet restricts the flow of traumatic bleeding and should be applied only when you're unable to stop the flow using other means. You should be able to apply a tourniquet on yourself or another party as a last resort.

First, make sure that the clothing has been removed from the wounded area and then tie the tourniquet 5 centimeters up from the wound site, leaving out a tab. Arteries are somewhat elastic, meaning that if severed they will retract slightly into the body. Since the artery must be pinched off, you must go up from the wound site to apply the tourniquet. Wrap tightly and then tie off the tourniquet. Note the time of application.

Once the tourniquet is put in place, it cannot be removed until the patient receives professional medical treatment. Removing the tourniquet may result in further arterial bleeding and fluid loss and then death because there is insufficient blood pressure for the heart to pump. On the other hand, the tourniquet will damage and eventually kill the tissue below its placement site. This is something you must

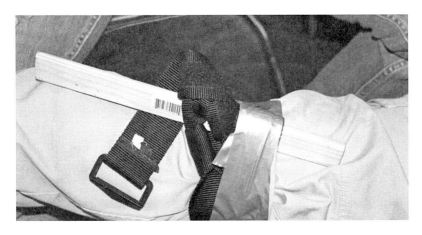

A tourniquet should be used as a last resort and can be improvised from a variety of common items, including belts, duct tape, scarves, and chains. Items to tighten the wrapping can include knives, pens, rulers, and sticks.

You might have to apply a tourniquet on yourself.

come to terms with when applying one. Without blood flow and oxygen and carbon exchange in the blood vessels, there will be irreparable damage. Typically the theme of "life over limb" is used when justifying the use of any type of tourniquet. There may be some individuals who would rather die than lose an arm or leg. Just know that applying a tourniquet could be a life-altering decision you are making for someone else.

The CAT (Combat

Application Tourniquet) is an excellent commercial product that I highly recommend. An improvised tourniquet can be made from a belt or strap and a stick. For a Russian tourniquet, tie a rope or cloth around the limb above the wound site. Turn the stick until the flow stops and then tie off tightly to prevent loosening.

Clearing the Airway

Once you have stopped the bleeding, you must clear the patient's airway. First, do a head tilt/chin lift. With one hand on the patient's chin and the other on his forehead, gently rock the head back. Next, turn the head and then finger-sweep the mouth and throat to clear any debris from the airway.

If the insertion of an airway device is needed to keep the airway open, place the size 3 device into the mouth to the side and turn 90 degrees, inserting it until it touches the lips. A great alternative to the oral airway is the NPA, or nasopharyngeal airway. A size 28 is the standard for an adult male. An NPA is less likely to move during transport.

Ensuring Breathing

The general rule to determine whether a patient is breathing is "look, listen, and feel." *Look* at your patient's chest to see if it rises and falls, put your ear to the patient's mouth and *listen* for evidence of breathing, and place your ear near his mouth to determine whether you can *feel* his breath on your ear.

If the patient is not breathing, use a mask to seal around the mouth and nose and perform rescue breathing at a rate of one breath every five seconds. Continue either until the patient begins breathing on his own or medical help arrives.

Each team member should know how to use a handheld bag valve mask to provide ventilation for a patient who is not breathing while the paramedic is performing more advanced procedures. In your vehicle or facility, you may have more advanced equipment, such as IV fluids and drip sets, AMBO bag, oxygen for administration, or an epinephrine pen and other over-the-counter drugs.

As noted, do *not* administer CPR.

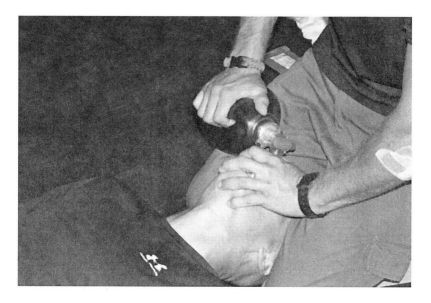

Every member of your crew should know how to use a bag valve mask (or Ambu) bag for nonbreathing patients.

Treating a Sucking Chest Wound

Treat a sucking chest wound with an improvised Asherman valve (the same thing as the commercial Asherman chest seal, or ACS), taping gauze on three sides to create a one-way valve. A sucking chest wound is a hole in the chest wall created by trauma (e.g., a gunshot or stab wound). It allows air to be sucked into the hole when the victim is inhaling. This air fills the pleural space between the lung and chest wall, thereby inhibiting lung inflation. This is dangerous because if a lung cannot inflate, there is insufficient oxygen exchange in the body. The other lung will compensate, but the pressure might increase and stress the undamaged lung. To minimize this pressure and pleural space inflation, you must seal the hole. Sealing the hole is simple; so do not try to "diagnose the problem." Simply treat what you see: the hole must be closed. Any hole in the anatomical area of the chest must be sealed, both entry and exit wounds.

To apply the chest seal (a commercial or an improvised one):

1. If it is available, use a Vaseline brand gauze pad sealed in a foil package.
2. Open the package and allow the gauze to stick to one side of the package (naturally, the one with the petroleum jelly).
3. Place the chest seal over the hole in the anatomical area of the chest, side, or back.
4. Using medical tape, duct tape, or gaffer tape, tape down on three sides only. This creates a one-way valve, meaning air can escape but does not get sucked in.
5. Place the patient in a semi-Fowler's position (elevate the upper body).

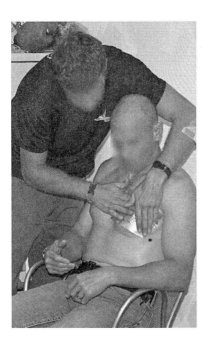 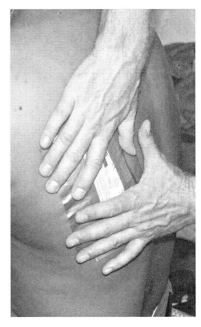

An Asherman valve can be placed over the hole of a patient with a sucking chest wound. The hole can be in the front or back.

Maintaining Body Temperature
Cover or expose the injured man from extreme cold or heat.
Place a blanket over him to protect from cold and shock. If he is in
the direct sun, block the rays using an improvised awning if possible.
Try to keep the patient dry by protecting him from precipitation or by
removing wet clothing if advisable. If it is windy, try to protect the
patient from that as well.

Administering an IV
Each team member should know how to prepare an IV solution
in order to help the EMT, who will be preparing the vein for the solution. Teaching each man on your security team how to start and
administer an IV is ideal if time allows for the proper training of such

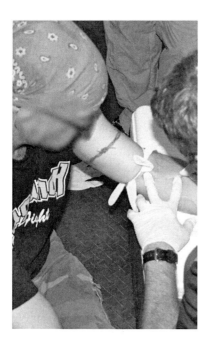 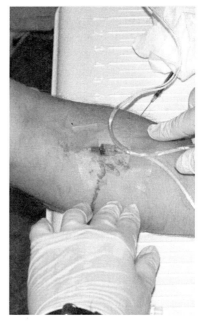

Administering an IV in the field.

techniques. The IV fluids and drip set should be readily available in the vehicle and facility trauma kits.

Dealing with a Severed Appendage

If a finger or other body part is severed, then it must be preserved if you have any hopes of reattaching it. The best thing to do is to wrap the part in a plastic bag or wrap it in plastic, a towel, or piece of clothing before placing it in a cold, dry location and transporting it with the patient to the hospital. Examples of storage places are a bowl of ice, a cooler, or the air conditioning vent of a car if that is all you have. The cold will do the following:

- Slow the blood flow
- Prevent or slow bacteria growth
- Reduce oxygen consumption
- Delay tissue death in the body part

FIRST AID EQUIPMENT

In addition to basic equipment carried by each security warrior (outlined in Chapter 5), the following medical gear should be available to team members:

- Tourniquet
- 4x4 HemCon dressing
- Asherman valve
- Size 3 airway device
- Small ACE bandage

The gear should be wrapped in cellophane to keep it together and clean, and should be carried

An example of a field medical kit a team should have with it at all times, whether in a car or at home base.

by each team member. More elaborate kits should be kept in the vehicle or base facility. The security warriors cannot be weighted down with any equipment that will hinder their ability to fight. All team members must be familiar with all the kit contains and each item's usage and indication.

TRAUMA SCENARIOS

Below are a few examples of operational scenarios that are likely in security work. Each member of your team must be prepared to handle each type of scenario. What would *you* do in each case?

Scenario 1
The undercover man is shot in an extremity from behind cover. He is conscious and needs a tourniquet and first aid dressing.

Scenario 2
A uniformed man is shot in his extremity and isn't breathing. He needs rescue breathing and a tourniquet.

Scenario 3
An undercover man is stabbed in the chest and is breathing but is not conscious. He needs an Asherman valve.

Scenario 4
A uniformed man is shot in the head, shoulder, and neck. He is breathing but needs a first aid dressing, HemCon bandage, and ACE bandage.

Scenario 5
An undercover man is shot in two extremities and requires two tourniquets, one of which must be improvised.

One great resource for medical training is your local community college. Most colleges have EMT programs that last about three months and can give you all the skills you need in the field and much more. There are specialized courses for advanced trauma life support and tactical combat casualty care, each lasting about a weekend. The key is to keep up with what you have learned. The best form of training for the security team is to hire a military combat medic and have him privately train the team for a week in trauma first aid. There is no need for paperwork or fancy certifications and titles—the skills to save lives will be enough in an emergency.

CHAPTER 11

Tactical Driving

In security work, you spend a considerable amount of time in vehicles, and often you're behind the wheel. Therefore, it is important that you become one with your machine, just as you become one with your weapon when it is in hand. Thus, each security warrior should have training in operational driving. This includes proficiency in high-speed accelerating, cornering, braking, ramming, using hand brake turns for changing direction, driving off-road, navigating on wet or snowy surfaces, evading obstacles, using a manual transmission, firing from a vehicle while it's moving, and driving with night vision equipment. It will take about a week to teach these skills at a beginner's level during the training course. This training course should be refreshed for one full day every six months.

TRAINING COURSES

I would highly recommend starting off with a quality rally-driving course to learn vehicle dynamics over uneven and various surfaces, such as gravel, ice, sand, or rain. Train using vehicles most similar to those you will use in the performance of your duty.

The next type of training you should seek is a basic off-road driving course. Learn how to drive over, around, or through such obstacles

An off-road driving course should teach you how to use 4x4s to cover rugged driving terrain.

as deep water, fallen trees, mud, and sand, as well as how to rock crawl. Learn how to get a vehicle unstuck and moving again by using tow straps, a wench, and pulley systems.

Once you learn how to drive fast and off-road, a specialty security-driving course is in order. This course should focus on the security aspects of driving in tandem, the most secure formations, antiambush and escape procedures, and firing from moving and stationary vehicles from various positions. One school I know of is Team O'Neil out of New Hampshire, but there are many other reputable ones that you can research.

Before taking off, the driver will adjust the controls, seats, and mirrors to his fit and personal preferences. In general, it is a good idea to have a designated wheelman who concerns himself with just that. It can be a member of your team who performs the duty of chauffeur for the day.

As with any possible confrontation, your best option is avoidance. Passing barriers and obstacles should be emphasized in the evasive-driving element of training. You also need to learn how to defend your vehicle once a situation is no longer evadable. The old adage "the best defense is a strong offense" applies equally in tactical driving scenarios, so you'll need to master offensive driving techniques for those times when you must go on the offensive in your vehicle. One of the main skills you will need is ramming. A key element to an ambush is the "stopper" that halts your movement in order for you to be attacked. If you can avoid or defeat the stopper, then the ambush can be avoided or defeated. Ramming or pushing your way out of a situation is surely better than fighting your way though it.

VEHICLE SELECTION

Vehicle selection is an important consideration in tactical driving. Before you can select the right vehicle for your mission, you must do a threat assessment to determine what equipment you need on your vehicle. The first safety feature to consider on your vehicle is armor, as well as a self-healing, puncture-proof gas tank.

For example, the U.S. Secret Service opts for a tank that looks like a car. The Cadillacs they use are hardly cars at all, built on a special-purpose frame and fitted with ordinary Cadillac body panels and badging. The glass is as thick a phone book, and the doors weigh more than 100 pounds. The Secret Service doesn't need agility—it needs armor. It always has two of these wherever its agents go because one may fail the safety checks performed before departure.

Armor

Do you need armor on your vehicle and, if so, how much? The VIP car needs to be bulletproof, but you must strike a balance between agility and penetration. Armor is the best security measure in hostile environments, but it will greatly hamper your vehicle's ability to maneuver, be evasive, or go off-road.

The first areas to armor on a car are the windows because they are the most likely points of attack and armoring them with bulletproof glass protects the head and upper body from attack. Armoring the doors and entire passenger compartment is another option to protect against grenades and other explosives. Other key points to protect are the radiator, fuel cell, undercarriage, and roof.

A simple way to think of armor is penetration versus agility.

This security detail is definitely in a dangerous setting. Armoring this vehicle would probably be a good idea, as protecting staff and passengers is more critical than being able to maneuver easily.

An armored undercover van is essential when moving people in certain areas of the world, such as the Middle East, Africa, or South America.

More armor means less agility. You can't have both. In a truly hostile environment, such as Africa and the Middle East, armoring is more important. In some cases it is more important for your vehicle to blend in with those commonly seen in a particular region than to be armored. There is an outstanding factory-armored BMW 7 series that offers an excellent mix of agility and armor, but it does stand out and has zero off-road application.

Other Safety Features
The car should have its own air supply built in to avoid toxic fumes that could be sprayed or thrown in grenade form at the car.

It should also be equipped with its own nozzles to spray pepper spray, oleoresin capsicum (OC), or Mace in case of a mob attacking the vehicle. The windows in the backseat, where the VIP traditionally sits, should be tinted or otherwise covered so that you can see out, but an attacker or sniper doesn't have a clear shot at your passenger.

Run-flat tires designed to resist punctures and to be driven at reduced speeds or for limited distances even if punctured are a must for escaping ambushes as well.

NAVIGATION

Learning how to navigate by using municipal and traffic maps is essential for figuring out routes and understanding the area where you will be working. Do not bother with GPS devices. GPS more often than not will fail or prove unreliable. Depending on GPS means that in an emergency you may be left staring at a blank computer screen. What if your device breaks, gets wet, loses power, or is simply wrong? The best thing you can do is print a map off the Internet; you know its level of relevance and how up to date it is. GPS devices need constant updating and are not for security-minded programs or agencies.

Next memorize your environment and your commonly used routes of travel and possible travel alternatives. Rely on your maps and your memory, and forget GPS.

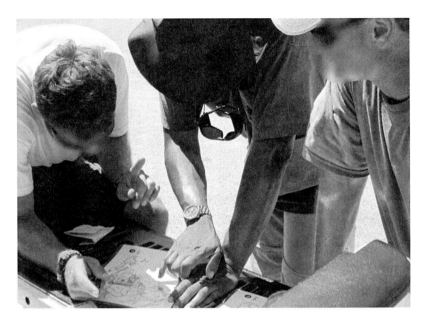

This team plots an open-field land-navigation course using a map marked with detours, alternate routes to destination, known vulnerable points, and safe havens.

Selecting the route and reconnaissance to avoid danger points and threats is everyone's responsibility, but primarily the wheelman and vehicle/convoy commander ultimately decides on the routes. Remember, map reading is your first step in building your battle plan while on the road. Find the most direct route from A to B and then map out all the alternative routes. Next find all the route vulnerabilities, such as tunnels, bridges, turns without visual contact with the other side, rolling hills, and remote areas lacking population and movement. To identify choke points, search for possible spots you would target if you were the attacker/ambusher. That's why experience as a soldier and warrior is so important: you can be your own devil's advocate. Have a plan for all route detours and alternate routes. Know where the nearest hospitals and police stations are. It is

All routes must be planned in advance and checked throughout the trip for changes and possible disruptions.

faster to drive to the hospital or police station than to call and wait.

Your most vulnerable points throughout the day will be those times when you are not in a secure structure. This means that any travel is dangerous. So carefully calculate your route. Drive it first, test everything, and micromanage all the details, no matter how small.

Last but not least, always make sure you and your passengers are buckled up. You can't fight if you're too injured to do so after a crash. If your car crashes or gets into an accident, be suspicious. Drive to a police station, fire station, army base, or hospital. *When there is a doubt, there is no doubt.* This means that if you doubt some circumstance is genuine, don't doubt your intuition—move out! Have a set protocol for problems en route, such as flat tires, empty fuel tanks, minor crashes, police road-blocks, and traffic stops. Know when you need to alter your route and where you will go. If you are stationary too long, you become vulnerable and need to set up a perimeter and call in the backup vehicles in your convoy to continue with the protected parties.

PART THREE

SKILLS

All the training that you complete is worthless unless it gives you the requisite skills, procedures, and protocols you need to do your job. This section covers some of the specialized skills a security warrior must master to perform the many functions involved in security work. Of course, each security operation will have its own list of specific skills, procedures, and protocols for security warriors.

CHAPTER 12

Undercover Security Skills

Undercover operators must have the skills to work proactively. They must develop the ability to blend in with the people around them so they have the opportunity to see things that someone in uniform would not, since uniformed people are treated differently, especially by the bad guys. This allows undercover operators to assess situations candidly. Law enforcement agencies depend on undercover operations, and so should you. They are essential to a good security team. No matter what the mission, undercover and covert security allows your team to ambush the attackers.

If terrorists or criminals can identify the bodyguards right off the bat, then that is whom they will take out first. A suit and an earpiece aren't the best look for working in the civilian sector. You want to be security, not appear to be security. What an undercover security agent does is act as an invisible bodyguard, making himself less of a target and more of a security operator. Having an undercover presence allows security teams to go on the offensive. Being undercover allows you to respond to a stimulus more effectively than can a uniformed guard because you have the element of surprise on your side.

An undercover operator can be "disguised" while not being in any disguise at all. To accomplish this, simply dress in clothing or items that look innocuous but are purposefully chosen to make the wearer blend in. For example, you can have an iPod with ear buds,

In this training photo, members of an undercover operations team cover as a teammate is loaded into the vehicle.

but not have the musical device turned on. This way, most people will assume that you're listening to music and not their conversation, so they will speak more freely. Plus, it will deter people from approaching or distracting you with questions.

An undercover operator should act like everyone else around him. Thus, you can use such things as a cell phone with a camera to take pictures, whereas a uniformed man can't do so without looking suspicious or unprofessional. You can get extremely close to a suspicious person without having him feel threatened. With dark sunglasses on, you can stare directly at someone and still look like you're not, whereas uniformed personnel can't do this without raising suspicion.

There are four primary ways in which undercover operators contribute to a security system:

1. Contain and protect the inner circle from the unwanted element by constantly scanning the most vulnerable areas for a potential attack to prevent it from occurring.
2. Pass along relevant information to the inner circle.
3. Respond more quickly to a stimulus than anyone else in the inner circle.

4. Prevent further damage in a crisis. He keeps people out of a freshly opened sterile area and provides local law enforcement with a concise account of what happened when they arrive.

The true test of a well-trained undercover agent is the way he reacts in a crisis. While undercover, you must react quickly and decisively because that can determine the outcome of the entire situation. First you're alerted to a possible threat by a sight or sound. Whatever this threat stimulus is, you assess it and determine its danger level. At this point, it is your job to decide whether to react to the threat. If you observe both means and motivation from this particular threat, you will definitely react. For example, if you see someone armed with a knife running in the direction of innocent people, you act immediately.

Conversely, you wouldn't react to a mugging or a robbery outside the immediate vicinity. As an undercover operative, you must be focused on your mission; you can't allow yourself to be easily distracted by unrelated events, or easily set up by suspicious parties. You're trained to ignore an action that is far enough away to not be a threat to the person or place being guarded. Allowing your attention to be drawn away to a distant situation might actually result in harm to the very person or place you're paid to protect. You do report the unrelated occurrence to the HQ communication room and let the people in charge decide what to do with it. It is up to them; you must stay focused.

Once you decide to react, you transform yourself into a machine. In a crowded situation, you must be fast and accurate. You move like a programmed robot that does its job without emotion until the job is finished. At this point, you draw your weapon and close in on the target as fast as possible, firing when able. The last shot will be to neutralize the target. You then do a quick search in the direction from which the threat originated for more enemies, weapons, or bombs. Immediately after the encounter, you communicate the status of the current situation to the prescribed person in the war room or HQ communication center. You then retreat to a position of cover (a tactical position), where you watch for further threats until backup arrives.

A tactical position is one in which you can see the enemy, have cover from incoming fire or blast, shoot back and return fire, have control of your area of responsibility, respond and help other security emergencies in the vicinity, and communicate effectively.

Undercover work is a tool, not an end in itself. Some basics of undercover work to remember include:

- Dress like the locals, in accordance with local customs and climate.
- Do what the locals are doing, whether waiting with a bag for a cab or bus or sitting at a restaurant sipping a coffee.
- You must appear to be a local in every way until you have to break cover to react to a threat.
- Use a cell phone for communication with HQ so that you look like any civilian chatting on the phone.
- Do not use cheap earpieces because they are cumbersome and obvious.
- Eye contact and other gestures are more acceptable in some cultures than others. Remember, you are not following someone, but rather profiling everyone. Even in certain areas of the United States (e.g., on the subways in New York City), eye contact is seen as challenging.
- No flying solo. Work in teams of two or more.
- Have a well-rehearsed backstory to satisfy basic questions you might be asked. Make sure that your teammates and you are consistent with your stories and details.
- Two undercover men can play off each other and seem more natural than a lone security agent.
- Use your cell phone to take photographs of people, cars, and license plates. E-mail them back to HQ for analysis.
- Use sunglasses and head phones (off) to deter people from approaching or speaking to you. This prevents you from getting distracted and will make you seem more irrelevant and less conspicuous.

CHAPTER 13:

Searching Techniques

It was September 2011. I had been out of the IDF for 20 months at this point. Over that time period, I had been working in the security consulting field, mostly training and some VIP security work. I was busy every week running a course somewhere in the world. Work was nonstop, and I found myself on a plane at least four times a month. I even had a stretch of two months where I never slept at home—every week I would fly to another city and run a training course there. I quickly realized something: I was not teaching Israeli combat shooting or Israeli instinctive shooting or an IDF rifle course or anything of the sort. What I was teaching was a crash course on the Israeli combat mindset, with the pistol, rifle, or active shooter. This is what I have tried to impart, as best as I can through written text, in this book.

I found myself teaching this course in Florida, Alaska, Kentucky, Texas, Pennsylvania, Nevada, Georgia, Missouri, Louisiana, and New York, as well as in Canada, Italy, and Israel, and that's just off the top of my head. The number of people I trained in 2010 alone easily exceeded 600. I worked with members of the following groups:

- TSA's Federal Flight Deck Officers
- Royal Canadian Mounted Police

- Federal Bureau of Prisons/Department of Justice
- NATO
- Italian police (Carabinieri)
- New York Police Department
- Alaska State Troopers SWAT Team
- Hollywood (FL) SWAT Team
- Texas Department of Public Safety
- Round Rock (TX) Police Department
- Austin (TX) Police Department
- Plantation (FL) Police Department
- Anchorage (AK) Police Department SWAT Team
- Georgia State Police
- Suffolk County (NY) Police Department
- Chester County (PA) Sheriff's Office

And this list does not include all private security companies and civilians for whom I worked.

But this was training, not *doing*. From time to time I would get an e-mail or a phone call about a protection or security detail. If I found it interesting, I would do it; if not, then I would pass. In my opinion, there is nothing worse than going into a security job just for the money. If that is the case, then how can you possibly take the safety of those you are protecting seriously?

The following job came across my desk from a colleague who passed it on to me. The mission was to protect a double agent who was living in the United States under political asylum from the State Department. His name was Mosab Hassan Yousef, and he had been a spy for the Israeli intelligence establishment for 10 years. Yousef, the son of Sheikh Hassan Yousef—one of the founders of Hamas—had written a book, *Son of Hamas*, about his experiences.

In this case, Yousef had been invited to give a speech to a group of about 300 people in downtown Miami on September 15, 2011. It was my job to make sure that the event occurred without incident. I quickly assembled my team of former Israeli operatives, who all felt that protecting this spy for Israel was an honor. We assembled our battle plan: we visited the facility, spoke to all the facility staff, studied all the participants on the guest list, created contingency plans in case of attack. In short, we took no chances. This man was on the top of Hamas' most-wanted list, and he *wasn't* getting killed on my watch.

When the day of the event rolled around, we were ready—all possibilities had been accounted for, and everything was running smoothly. We even had two undercover agents from the City of Miami's Close Protection Unit liaising with us for the mission, and they were very professional. All the guests were seated, and all my people were in place, ready for Yousef to come in.

Just then the building manager and security found me and complained about our blocking the doors leading to the kitchen from the event hall. I had set up all the doors so that you could exit them but not come in through them unless you had a key. That is, all doors

The author (standing right) and his team provide protection for Mosab Hassan Yousef, the son of Sheikh Hassan Yousef, one of the founders of Hamas.

except the kitchen doors, which were saloon-style doors that could not be locked. So I had blocked them by stacking tables and chairs up and then covering them with a curtain. This would make entrance from that point noisy and slow. I also had one of the Miami officers at that entrance. The hotel personnel complained that this created a fire hazard and, thus, the entrance could not be blocked. I countered that the door did not say "EXIT" above it and the kitchen had too many access points for me to control all of them. I sent one of my best men to deal with the issue while I remained in place, anticipating that at any minute I would be alerted that the party was in the staging area outside and ready to enter the garage.

My second in command explained to the building staff that Hamas was a ruthless terrorist organization and Yousef had spied on it for years. He told them that Yousef had risked his life to save lives and preserve Western values, and that Hamas wanted him dead. "We will not let that happen," he promised them.

The hotel security guy almost fell over backward and exclaimed, "We are not equipped to deal with such a guest!" We advised him to sit tight—in two hours, it would all be over.

In the meantime, the Miami guys and I went to the back garage, where the driver was waiting to bring Yousef right up to the door so he could make an easy entrance and exit. This garage was adjacent to the back door of the event hall, which was empty. We decided to do one more search and sweep of the area before we called Yousef up. Remember, Yousef was most vulnerable while moving from the car (a sterile zone) to the structure (another sterile zone). When we searched the area, one of the Miami guys found a car parked sideways across two parking spots, with a backpack on the seat and wires sticking out of it, a plug in a cigarette lighter, and a cell phone on top. I saw it and knew exactly what we needed to do. First I tried to call my driver to tell him to remain in the staging area, but he failed to answer. Then I had one of the Miami guys run the plate and get a name and photo. I sent the other to contact the building staff to see if the owner of the vehicle worked at the hotel. The other was to hold the line in the event hall and be ready for an evacuation.

My driver was in a Porsche turbo, and I could hear the motor roaring as it climbed the parking garage ramps at 8:00 P.M. I started to run down the ramps, hearing the engine getting closer. When he rounded the corner and saw me running in the empty garage, he stopped. I told him to head out, that it was not safe. In the meantime, my second was back from dealing with the kitchen staff, and I briefed him. The Miami guys had a name and a photo of the owner of the car, but no one knew him. We send a unit to go by the address on the vehicle registration to check it out and see if the car was stolen.

Two uniformed Miami-Dade Police Department officers showed up with the security guy involved in the earlier kitchen incident. They started to ask some strange questions about us. All the while, 300 people were waiting inside for the speaker to appear. My guys were keeping it cool in there while one of the City of Miami guys was still working the identity case. My second went to the staging area as a backup for the driver. The two uniforms said they had received a call from building security that "there may be people with guns here," and naturally they wanted to see what was going on.

I looked at he building security guy and asked, "Did you call the cops on us?" He said that he had because "I didn't understand what was going on." Just then the City of Miami Close Protection officer flashed his ID and politely told the uniforms to beat it, and they did.

I was telling the other Miami officer to start evacuating the people when the garage manager came running up to say he had found out who owned the car. It belonged to the person who takes the money at the exit gate of the parking garage. We ordered him up. He came and opened the car for us. Apparently he was living out of his car in the lot, and the electronics were his laptop and cell phone. We brought in Yousef, and all went well.

The moral of this story is that we did what we had to. We checked and double-checked. And that is what you must do. Be vigilant and follow your lists and protocols.

• • •

Before the hunted can be found, a search must take place. Because of the way terrorists operate in modern-day society, this search must include everyone and everything. There are no direct trails to terrorists; thus you must search every person, suspicious or not, before deeming an area sterile.

Why must security teams search? Because searching allows the team to go on the offensive. There are specific procedures and protocols that define what is suspicious and what is worth searching. Everything that passes a security warrior gets checked, although what you're looking for and how in depth the search must be vary according to the circumstances of your environment and security situation.

When you search an area or a perimeter, check out both the interior and the exterior of the structure. You do this automatically when you arrive on scene. You should always stay in front of the person you're protecting so that you search an area before he enters it. This is called *advance work*. The earlier you do this, the safer your VIP will be. It could be a recon on a parking lot, a hotel meeting room, a restaurant, or even just around a corner.

There are four basic types of searches that you will partake in as a security warrior:

- Search and leave
- Search and lock
- Search and stay
- Search and check

SEARCH AND LEAVE

The most basic form of search is the "search and leave," an apt description of what you do during this hunt. This search revolves around the security personnel checking an area that isn't part of the locale you're guarding just to make sure nothing suspicious is going on inside. The search area isn't your priority, but it must be safe because it could affect the safety of the person or place you're guarding. An example of this might be a bathroom in a facility into which you're escorting your client. Once you've searched this area, you leave and don't go back.

SEARCH AND LOCK

The "search and lock" involves searching an area and then locking it behind you. This type of search is relevant for a room or sealable area that you can lock up securely after searching. You have the key to this room; thus you're in control of anything or anyone that enters and exits it after it has been deemed sterile. An example of this might be a storage facility, garage, or another area generally not entered.

SEARCH AND STAY

The "search and stay" is a good way to control an area when working undercover. This method of searching allows you to be in full control of your environment without exposure unless absolutely necessary. When you arrive on scene in a new area, house, or government building, you ensure that you have full control of, and responsibility over, the area. You must make it your own. To do this, you start by doing a visual search. Inspect all areas of a potential threat, to include people of interest. Search all corners, bushes, containers, and cubbies. Look under benches, behind walls, in tool sheds, inside trash cans, and at any other places a bomb or weapon might be stashed. Try to search in an inconspicuous manner so as not to alarm the public, but be thorough.

An example of a search and stay is to check the public area you're responsible for—such as newspaper machines, car windows, trash cans—and then remain on scene to notice any unusual activity that might take place, such as in a parking garage before a VIP arrives.

Again, being undercover limits your searching thoroughness. You don't want to expose yourself by obviously searching the area, so you discreetly look for more obvious objects and people. Being in control of an area requires that you look at every unknown area in the zone you're working. An example of this would be looking behind a bush or inspecting a sleeping bum to make sure it/he isn't a threat to the environment.

Once the search has taken place, it is essential to stay in the vicinity you have searched. You want to appear natural and to blend in. It is now your job to feed intelligence for the duration of the shift, but to do so in such a way that doesn't call attention to yourself.

SEARCH AND CHECK

The "search and check" is similar to the search and stay, except that the former is done overtly by one or more uniformed officers, and the public will witness this inspection. This check involves searching a physical area and, after it is determined secure, checking each individual who enters the designated area. Use a metal detector for special events, meetings, book signings, and other such situations. Check IDs and, most important, utilize behavioral analysis to detect suspicious people. This means that the metal detector is just a subterfuge to stimulate the people being screened. The one wanding is only there to act as a stimulator, while off to the side is a warrior observing the reactions and attitudes of the people being searched. This is the real check. A few examples of where this form of security is used are courthouses, shopping malls, and airports. In this specific type of search procedure, the security staff will arrive on scene in uniform to search the area they are assigned and open what is known as a *sterile zone*. Once it is deemed sterile, the security staff can be assured that the area is free of weapons and explosives.

The reason for searching the perimeter of any facility is to make sure there are no unknowns. That is your job as a security warrior. You must be able to guarantee that the area is under your control and is safe.

CHAPTER 14

Interrogation Techniques

When searching people and their property, you usually have to ask the individuals involved questions, or interrogate them. The interrogation should be conducted with direction and purpose. During the questioning process, the interviewer will run into four main problems: location, time, compliance, and identification.

The *location* is critical when questioning people because they might respond differently in private as they do when they are with others. Also you can get a better feel for the person and situation when you have a more personal setting. A line of people waiting to get into a sterile zone is not a good location for questioning.

Time is a factor because usually you have only a limited amount of it in which to question each person. You need to assess whether that person is a threat and that's it; either let him go or apprehend and detain him. Twenty minutes per person is the maximum amount of time this should take in a closed space off to the side.

Compliance is an issue because some people will be naturally resistant to others seeing their identity documents and to answering questions. A person's noncompliance doesn't signify guilt; it simply means you have to work harder to get the desired result. A completely noncompliant person should be treated as suspicious and should not be permitted to enter the sterile area until he has been properly identified.

Finally, there is the problem of *identification*. There are many fake IDs that look real and will pass most security inspections. Some modern fake IDs will even have legitimate numbers and bar codes and be readable by machines. This is where your interrogation skills come in. You must ask the right identity questions to determine whether the individual's story matches his identity documents. He must also account for his belongings and anyone accompanying him.

To maximize your 20-minute questioning window, it is best to ask questions focused on two things: time and place. The time line of events and the location of events for given times may reveal a lie or a fabricated story. For practice, ask a friend questions based on time and location. Your friend's job is to make every answer a lie but to follow a story that is believable. For example, pretend you're questioning a man trying to enter an office building that is being guarded because of VIPs inside. Remember, all fabricated stories will fall apart with time and place.

When interviewing someone, remember that you never give away information. Never say, "I need to ask because we have a VIP coming at noon, and everyone is being checked out." Just politely say, "I need to ask you a few questions before I can let you in," and start reading his reactions to your questions. Don't accuse the person you're questioning of lying or tell him that he is suspicious, as this could be counterproductive. Use pressure only as a last resort, and pressure with an open-ended question. For example, "You arrived on bus number 4, but that bus doesn't start its run until 4:00 P.M., and it's just now 10 A.M.?"

Think outside the box and match your speech to the situation and the person you're interviewing. Address a businessman as "sir" not "dude," while a 16-year-old boy is "young man." It is important to write down the answers people give to your questions because you may need them for follow-up questions, and you don't want to confuse a current story with stories you heard 15 minutes ago. Speak with confidence and don't repeat questions. Always follow a format of open-ended questions leading to more open-ended ones (question-answer-question-answer). Whoever is with the person is questioned separately to check consistency of the stories. Again, checking identification, searching, and interviewing are skills each warrior must possess, but using a professional checker for questioning is most effective.

QUESTIONING INTERNATIONAL AGENTS

There is one group on whom your interrogation techniques might not work. Agents of international espionage are everywhere and have very strong and supported backstories. They will have "real" fake IDs that will pass even the toughest checks. Your job is to reduce their ability to gather information for future attacks as much as possible. That means keeping them away from your facility by denying them access.

To comprehend the weaknesses and difficulties you will encounter with such a spy, as well as the vulnerabilities he will take advantage of, you must "become the spy." It is necessary to enter the mind of the enemy in order to fully understand how to defeat him. To do this, you must leave the facility and take a few hours to gather as much information as possible that would help an outsider infiltrate your security system, as this is the only way to understand and defend potential weak points.

The good news is that a foreign intelligence man is just that, foreign. So he is more likely to stand out if scrutinized or interrogated. Like a Canadian in Miami, he will be spotted as different, even if the differences are subtler than, say, an African in Asia. This person might be the best intelligence operator, but his appearance is still a liability. The spy might hesitate to act on an opportunity if he isn't confident of his ability to blend with his surroundings. Also, he subconsciously thinks he is under security surveillance and suspicion, which also will affect his proficiency, movements, and progress.

When a foreign agent is observing an installation, he is looking for specific details, and the security staff needs to be familiar with what he is looking for. Primarily he is gathering information on two main things: the facility itself and the people who frequent it. Of primary interest to him are the schedules of the security staff, such as when guard shifts begin and end. He will also try to establish what time other personnel arrive at the facility. Most important, he is interested in ascertaining the response times of the security element to a threat or an inquisitive civilian.

Any information about the types of weapons used and other surveillance equipment is important as well. The dress and procedures of the security detail will also be closely observed. Finally, the structure of the actual facility will be under scrutiny and very hard to defend from observation. The enemy will relay whatever intelligence he can gather on the number of staff, weapons, stories, barriers, buildings, vehicles, gates, cameras, and walls, as well as distances, schedules, and reaction times, to his personnel so they can use it to plan the most detailed attack plan possible.

Trained foreign intelligence operatives are among the hardest to detect. It requires trained security checkers who know what to look for and what questions to ask to keep the operatives out of your secured facility and away from your client. They might send a paid stool pigeon to make trouble or look overtly suspicious in order to watch how your team reacts to the threat and how long it takes them to respond and react to the party in question.

PART FOUR

THREAT ASSESSMENT AND RESPONSE

Without threats, there would be no need for security personnel. A person or place is protected because of some perceived or real risk. It is your job as a security professional to be able to assess the threat level accurately and respond to the threat while making sure that the installation remains secure. Among the possible threats that you may have to defend against are bombs, suicide bombers, ambushes, and hostage-taker scenarios. This section tells you what you need to know to do this.

CHAPTER 15

Threat Levels

In security work there are three threat levels. In ascending order, they are Level A, Level B, and Level C.

LEVEL A

A Level A threat means that someone requires further investigation, but you don't necessarily see any means or motivation present. A suspicious person would be considered a Level A threat. You must either approach the person and make inquiries, report him to another person of authority, or open a sterile area around him. The most you can do to this person is physically force him to leave, search him, or draw your weapon on him to make him obey commands. You can't shoot him, as he isn't a confirmed threat. The presence of means or motivation—but not both—characterizes a Level A threat.

LEVEL B

You must react to all Level B threats and removed from the area. Any attack on a structure or the people inside is considered a Level B threat. A person across the street with a knife is a threat, but not an immediate one because it will take time for him to do damage and escalate to Level C. A threat remains Level B until the use of immediate deadly force is absolutely necessary to prevent an imminent attack.

For a Level B threat, you can fire in the air to try to stop the person; if this fails, then shoot the would-be attacker's legs to prevent escalation. A person *suspected* of being a bomber would be a Level B. You can't kill a Level B until you're certain of the imminent threat; you can only take appropriate action to force the threat to comply, thereby preventing escalation to Level C.

LEVEL C

A Level C threat is the highest category and requires immediate neutralization. It represents an immediate threat to the lives of people you're protecting, and you can only destroy this threat with the use of deadly force.

As a security warrior, you must have the authority to conduct brief investigations on all suspicious activities, whether Level A, B, or C. The authority will be different, depending on the area being worked. Generally, this authority includes the ability to search, question, detain, confiscate, and arrest. You must have this authority to help assess how threatening the suspicious person is. Once the threat level is determined, the person should be arrested and detained until the local police arrive and take it from there. Security warriors suppress the problem until local police officers arrive, after being called by central command at dispatch.

CHAPTER 16

Defending a Facility

The security team will face several types of threats, but all can be categorized into four basic categories: espionage, crime, civil unrest, and terror. The key is to identify what threats fall into which categories so that you will be better equipped to deal with them when they arise. These four types of threats can present themselves at any time, and categorizing them in that moment is not practical. Know the threats and their most common forms, and then build a protocol for each to help you better defend your facility.

ESPIONAGE

Security teams must protect against intelligence gathering or espionage from the potential attacker. They can detect photographers, videographers, and people gathering information and stop them. This is accomplished most effectively with the use of undercover security.

While you're working to stop the intelligence gatherers, they may be testing you. They may send someone who is obviously suspicious looking into the outer circle to get security personnel to react, thereby exposing undercover operators or your protocols for reacting to suspicious personnel. They will record the reaction time it takes for security element to react. It is crucial for the security team to detect these intelligence gatherers in the outer circle and eliminate them so that the sterile area around the protected space/person is maintained.

CRIME

Theft and vandalism are two of the main criminal activities that all societies face, and having a vigilant outer-circle defense can prevent them from becoming a problem inside your security perimeter.

CIVIL UNREST

Protests or riots may not seem like much of a threat to your security operations, but they must be controlled and monitored because they have the potential to erupt and threaten your facility and its occupants. As long as the protest or riot doesn't penetrate the middle circle and is confined to a public area and under police control, it isn't a danger to the security staff. However, security personnel in the outer circle must watch the situation and prepare for how they will handle the mob if rioters attempt to attack your facility. Civil unrest may result from the political climate, natural disaster, or a similar occurrence.

TERROR

The last type of threat to the security team involves the most dangerous and most effective type of enemy: the terrorist. He is the most difficult to stop and requires the highest level of vigilance.

Terrorism can strike anytime, anywhere, and can appear to be nothing at all until it is too late. Terrorism can come in the form of a sniper, a drive-by shooter, a suicide bomber, or perhaps a vehicle ramming into the facility. The different forms of terrorism are endless. The number-one characteristic that makes terrorists so difficult to deal with is that the terrorist doesn't usually give up until his mission is accomplished. He wants to move in, attack, and do as much damage as possible no matter what the cost. He is motivated by hatred, religion, tribalism, or nationalism, or some other emotional element. Plus, he doesn't usually give up and run if he encounters opposition, as criminals often do.

The first person to encounter one of these four types of threats is the undercover operator on the outside circle. He will communicate his findings to the managers on the inner circle, which constitutes the last line of defense.

A reaction sequence is as follows:

- Stimuli by way of sound or sight
- Decision to act and how best to do so
- Closing distance to threat neutralization
- Quick search of immediate area
- Opening a sterile area
- Tactical position
- Communication

NOTE: The indicators for the number-two man to close distance and neutralize are the same indicators for the primary man to retreat with the protected to a secure location.

CIRCLES OF DEFENSE

When you're protecting a facility or a person, you have three lines of defense: the outer circle, middle circle, and inner circle. All the circles of defense are based on the maps, blueprints, and actual physical structure of the location you're defending.

Outer Circle

The outer circle is your first line of defense against security threats. It consists of things located beyond the obvious sterile area you have created around the person/facility you're protecting. Outer-circle defense consists of vehicle patrols around the streets in the area, undercover security personnel walking around in public, and

A fence can help secure the middle circle of a facility.

Part of your middle-circle security involves keeping a close watch around the perimeter and controlling who enters the facility.

video cameras documenting things that are across the street and hidden from plain sight.

Middle Circle

Between the outer circle and the inner circle lies a physical perimeter known as the middle circle. Some of the tools used by middle circle defenders are gates, fences, cameras, motion detectors, and perimeter patrols of the facility. Middle-circle guards may deal with people entering or leaving the facility or check people's IDs. Their function is observatory. If someone tries to penetrate the middle circle, he is suspicious by default. He has knowingly attempted to enter a place where he doesn't belong, and security staff should react accordingly. Check ID, the person, and then his belongings, in that order.

Inner Circle

If someone passes from the middle circle into the inner circle, he gets inside the sterile area and is usually no longer routinely checked or scrutinized by security. Inner-circle security personnel just assume that a person who has made it to the inner circle has been deemed nonthreatening by the outer and middle circle staff and is to be trusted.

This is a mistake. The inner circle should have checkers whose job is to identify and search people. Inner-circle personnel should have special equipment to detect weapons and explosives. There should be managers overseeing the operation of the checkers, and at least one security warrior is needed for each security checkpoint within this inner circle. This way the checkers can do their job comfortably and confidently. The main objective of inner-circle staff is to identify and search every single person who attempts to come in. *There are zero exceptions.*

SOP FOR ALL THREAT LEVELS

It is important to build protocols for your specific installation and implement standardized operating procedures for each situation and location. Each location has its own unique circumstances. Below are situations for which each facility should definitely have a plan as part of its general reaction protocols and standard operating procedures. Each staffer should know these protocols at all locations:

- Violent attack protocol
- Communication procedures
- Specific area descriptions and duties
- Rotation and change of guard procedures
- Maps and floor plans
- Medical supplies and emergency procedures/equipment/locations
- Fire, flood, earthquake, or other natural disasters procedures
- Search procedures for individual locations in or around facility
- Patrol routes and times
- Bomb discovery procedures based on location found
- Bomb threats
- Explosions
- Evacuation procedures
- Intruders
- Unexpected visitors or guests
- Civil unrest
- Spies, reporters, and photographers
- Special equipment
- Flat-tire protocols
- Medical emergencies
- Distinct time to ER and rescue response times for whatever issues the facility or convoy may have
- Ambush procedures
- Hostage protocols

This list could contain 50 items or more, and each item could easily have three pages of detailed explanations, diagrams, and photographs. Each man on the team needs to memorize protocols for his installation. Remember, the above list is generic; your facility has its own unique security needs.

CHAPTER 17

Bomb Threats

Responding to bomb threats is a big part of security work. Such threats must be handled carefully to minimize risk and tragedy on one hand and inconvenience on the other. As a general rule, bomb threats are of three main types: general, specific, and suicide bombers.

GENERAL THREATS

General threats are the most common type and are often harmless or have an ulterior motive. A general threat often sounds something like this, "There is a bomb in the building, and you have one hour to get out!" or "I have planted a bomb, and it will go off in 10 minutes!" These types of threats are general in description and are used as a means to upset progress and scare people, possibly as a prank or as revenge.

The security warrior must think outside the area. The protected people are in a sterile area that has been searched and is being guarded. Since this is the case, an attack would be most effective outside this sterile box. So if the building is evacuated in the next 10 minutes, then all the protected people or the individual VIPs will be in an unguarded area unsecured, making them more vulnerable than they were before. Suddenly, you have bigger problems: panic, snipers, mobs, traffic, fire, police, and other variables.

The team must trust the searches of each warrior in his specific zone. Trust the checkers, trust the cameras, and trust the use of a tight system to its fullest. An initial search was performed, and the facility has been guarded since that time. After a threat, each warrior does a quick search of his area for anything out of place and then reports to command for further instructions. You're counting on the initial search and the random searches and your presence to ensure the safety of your zone.

SPECIFIC THREATS

Specific threats are entirely different and need to be taken seriously. You need to have a battle plan in place specifically for your facility in case you receive a specific bomb threat. An example of a specific threat might be: "There is a bomb in the men's room on the third floor, and it will explode at exactly 12:20 P.M. if you don't . . ." or "There is enough C-4 in the garage to level the block—don't try to find it or . . ." This is specific in its claim and should be seen as much more serious. In this case the security staff must secure an exit other than the front door and protect the people as they evacuate, treating the route of evacuation as a new fighting territory. As a security warrior, you must be paranoid to be good at your job. You must open up a sterile area for people to escape. Furthermore, once a large group is dispersed into society, they are no longer a concentrated group and therefore are much less of a target.

It is the specificity of the threat and the introduction of an ultimatum that make this bomb threat even more serious. The person who takes the call might be a random employee of the facility or perhaps a trained dispatch operator. Whoever answers the phone call should play dumb to get the caller to divulge as much information as possible. Either way, it is important that you have a specific plan of action for your facility and the surrounding area and its threats. The possibility that the threat is all part of a bigger ambush plan can't be ignored. Plan, plan, plan, and use lists!

SUICIDE BOMBERS

When located in an area where suicide bombers are a real possibility, your facility must have an effective, easily implemented protocol for such an occurrence. And all personnel at the facility must be trained in those protocols so they know what to do instantly if a suicide bomber shows up.

When most people read or hear the term *suicide bomber*, a young Muslim man is what springs to mind. However, suicide bombers come in all forms in this day and age. For example, in Chechnya, women take on the rolls of suicide bombers while the men partake in more traditional combat against their enemies. It is important that you remember this when providing security at a protected facility. No one gets ruled out because of sex, age, or general appearance.

Certain signs are considered obvious red flags when detecting suicide bombers. In terms of physical presence, if the suicide bomber is a Muslim, he (or she) may look clean, well dressed, showered, and freshly shaven. This is due to the ritualistic preparation before the act in the Islamic religion. The person may be sweating profusely, acting nervous, or operating in a trance-like state so as not to respond to verbal stimuli. The suicide bomber will be appropriately dressed, so he doesn't seem out of place at your facility. He could be wearing a suit because the jacket allows him to hide the bomb. But the bomb could be in a bag, strapped onto a leg or torso, or hidden somewhere else.

These days people are dressing more casually, even in business environments. If someone is trying too hard to blend in, they will likely stand out. Look for telltale mannerisms: the inability to speak freely or converse coherently, nervous sweating, stress-induced fidgeting, or a trance-like preoccupation. If you have the slightest indication that someone is a bomber, act immediately. In this case, it is better to be safe than sorry.

- **Use the following protocol to deal with any suspected bomber.**

1. Identify the suspicious party based on signs (e.g., dress, appearance, response, actions, belongings) or intelligence.
2. Use the element of surprise to take the bomber down fast (it is your best option). An aggressive physical tackle may be your best option, as you can position him facedown and search his torso and waistline.
3. Search the suspect quickly and react instantly either by shooting to the head if a bomb is confirmed or by apologizing for the takedown and search if there is no bomb.
4. After killing the bomber, open a sterile area around him and keep everyone as far away as possible.
5. Take up a protected tactical position and radio in the situation and your needs: "Dispatch, Mike at facility. Bomber down— need bomb squad and backup. Lock down the red gate."

- **If the initial confrontation is verbal, you can't use the element of surprise. Use the following protocol.**

1. Engage the suspect verbally: "Excuse me," "Stop!" or "Can I help you, sir?"
2. If the suspect bolts into a crowd of people and you reasonably believe he has a bomb, draw your weapon and fire at his legs. Then open a sterile area around him and notify dispatch of the situation. Don't let the suspect get up or advance; if he tries to, fire at his legs again. You can't kill him until you have confirmation of the bomb.
3. Make him lift his shirt or coat so you can check for explosives from a distance and behind cover. (Remember, the bomb will have ball bearings, nails, or other types of shrapnel that, upon detonation, could be flung through the air quite a distance and can do a lot of damage to you or any bystanders.)

- **If the suspect won't engage verbally and refuses to stop, do the following:**

1. If he continues to advance, draw your weapon, charge, and threaten to fire if he doesn't stop.
2. If he runs, shoot at the legs (as in number 2 for verbal engagements above).
3. If he starts to run into a crowd after the warning, fire to disable his legs.
4. If he runs away, then chase him until he is far enough to not be a threat. Then report to command.

In terms of chasing a shooter, bomber, or any other threat to the person you're protecting, you should only do so when the situation demands it. And when it comes to the chase, the rules are different depending on whether you're protecting a facility or a person.

If your mission is to protect a structure, before engaging in a chase you must make sure there is another warrior to secure the facility, and you should chase no farther than two corners. Once your suspect rounds two street corners, then his gunfire, suicide bomb, or small explosive will be ineffective on your structure. It is important to remember that your job is that of a security warrior and not a police officer. If your structure is safe, your job is being done properly. Your duty is to protect the facility you're assigned to and leave the terrorist to the local authorities (whom you will contact only after your assigned actions are completed).

When you're guarding a person, you *never* chase the assailant. If a suicide bomber or other threat endangers your client, you leave with the protected man as soon as the initial threat has been neutralized. Move out ASAP.

CHAPTER 18

Ambushes

By definition, an ambush is a surprise attack. You become more vulnerable to being ambushed as you become more complacent. It is human nature to become less observant as time passes and no threats occur. Then, suddenly, you're ambushed when you least expect it. The best way to survive an ambush is to avoid one, and the key to avoiding an ambush is to stay alert at all times to any threat, abnormality, or coincidence.

An ambush has three basic parts. The first part is the *stop*, which can be anything that gets you to stop. It doesn't matter whether you're in a car and a kid on a bike darts out in front of you, you're on a run and a train passes in front of you, or you're on a horse and a car impedes your progress. The stop achieves just what it says: it gets you to halt motion (inhibiting your ability to escape) for a brief period during which you're vulnerable to an ambush.

The second part of the ambush is the *attack*. The attack will generally come from a side where there is cover and concealment. The attack will be violent and rapid. An ambush isn't meant to be a prolonged gun battle or fight. It is meant to take advantage of the element of surprise and to hit hard, lasting a maximum of two minutes. Firing by the attacker(s) will come from one of the sides a little ahead of or a little behind the target.

The last element in an ambush is the *back plug*. This is where a vehicle or object blocks you so that you can't escape by reversing directions. The back plug vehicle might also serve as the escape mechanism for the assailants. As a member of the security team, it is important for you to know how to spot this type of situation and thus avoid a gunfight or kidnapping.

AVOIDING OR COUNTERING AN AMBUSH

First, watch out for a follow car behind you. Your team should have its own follow car to avoid your being tailed, as well as a lead car to protect your forward progress. All drivers and team members should have the travel and alternate routes memorized. Your follow and lead cars should have additional firepower and men for backup if an ambush ensues. They also provide defense and limit exposure in intersections and other areas along the route by positioning themselves properly.

You should remain in constant communication with your follow and advance cars, whether it is by radio or cell phone. A few simple pieces of equipment installed in the vehicles can make following you more difficult. For example, a bin can be fitted under the rear bumper that will drop caltrops onto the road, disabling a following vehicle's tires, or the bin could contain oil, which when dumped would affect the chase car's traction. These things are cheap and easy to rig, and they may save your life or that of your client. Of course, if you have your own follow car, then it should be the one equipped with the bin so that it doesn't get disabled by your caltrops or oil.

Ramming your way through an ambush at a high speed is your best defense, not fighting your way out. When driving on a highway or road with a median, it is smart to drive along the median to block off one side from attack, while the advance car protects the front and another protects the exposed side and rear. The concept is similar to standing in an elevator, with the VIP in the corner and security elements facing out in front of him.

All lane changes should start with the follow car to control the flow

Counterambush training is essential to learning how to avoid or counter any attempted ambushes.

of cars coming into your lane. To do this smoothly, all drivers need to have the routes memorized and remain in constant communication. Don't follow too closely: when stopped at a traffic light, each car in the convoy should be able to see the tires of the car in front of it to ensure enough distance for an escape from a standstill or while moving. The dedicated lead vehicle travels about half a kilometer ahead of the principal vehicle. This is so the driver or navigator can see what is around an upcoming bend, over a bridge (most vulnerable), or over a hill to recognize an ambush or potential hazard. Lead time will vary, depending on the road, route, travel situation, and other mission-specific factors.

SECURITY WHILE ON FOOT

While most of your travel will be in vehicles, for security's sake, but the ambush-avoidance techniques discussed above are also applicable when walking on the street or traveling by other means. For example, you have an advance man half a block ahead on foot in the direction of travel, and his job is to thwart trouble before it starts, just like that of the lead vehicle. There will also be a follow man hanging back half a block to watch the rear for any pursuers or attempted attack from the rear.

Just like when using a follow car, having a man in tactical position who can see the whole picture is crucial when traveling on foot. There should also be one man who walks directly to the VIP's rear right (the 4:30 position), analogous to the person who sits in the back of the car with him. This man is the principal protective warrior on the team, and he remains in direct arm's-length contact at all times. Finally, just as there is a man sitting in the front seat next to the driver of a vehicle, there is a man who walks two steps to the front and left (the number-two man) of the client. Each man controls the area directly in his security zone. If there is insufficient staff to cover all these positions, then the roles are peeled down to the lone warrior, who positions himself at the VIP's right rear.

TEAM FUNCTIONS

Most of the time you will operate on a security team. But even though there is a team, in the event of an ambush, the concept of the lone warrior still applies. If an attack occurs at any location or time, whoever can will engage the enemy first and continue until the attempt is thwarted, irrespective of the actions of the others on the team.

If there is an ambush, the team members respond as follows:

- A single warrior will respond to the combat by moving out and retreating with the protected as soon as there is a safe opportunity to do so. For example, one safe opportunity would be when a target is down. In that case, he is not firing at you because he is suppressed.
- If you have a two-man detail, both will respond initially, and then one will close distance to neutralize the threat while the other retreats to a point of safety or cover with the VIP.

This sniper is zeroing his weapon to start training in a rock quarry.

- A three-man detail will function with the warrior closest to the VIP retreating with him after initial threat contact. The other two warriors will devastate the attackers and close distance. After neutralization, the team will have a point for convening together for movement or holdout. This may be a car for movement or the alcove in the street for cover until help arrives.

As the team grows in size, their duties and fields of fire will get narrower. But, remember, once the threat has been left or been eliminated, your team should think more about movement and less about neutralization.

In an ideal situation, you position countersnipers in key locations to spot a threat before it can be executed. The snipers can also assist the security warriors on the ground in taking out a threat. A trained sniper and spotter are invaluable assets to a security team.

CHAPTER 19

Hostage-Scenario Protocols

A hostage situation is the worst-case scenario a security team will face, short of an all-out massacre. Simply put, it is a situation in which the ball is in the terrorist's court, and you must act accordingly. As Westerners, we value human life above all else, and that puts us at a disadvantage when dealing with terrorists who don't. However, you do have some techniques you can employ that might affect the outcome of the situation with as few innocent lives lost as possible.

Before discussing any solutions, however, you must understand what a hostage situation is. In order to declare a hostage situation, five things must be present:

1. Hostage taker/terrorist
2. Weapons
3. Hostages
4. Physical separation between hostages and you
5. Demands from the hostage taker

First, a hostage taker (or hostage takers in many cases) must be present. Once you have the hostage takers, you then most likely have the second element: weapons. Without weapons, such as guns or explosives, the terrorist will have little chance of success against security forces and even against the hostages. So weapons are an essential element to a hostage crisis.

Third, by definition a hostage situation requires that there be people held against their will. The hostages are the bargaining chips for the terrorists and the focus of the incident. As a general rule, the hostages can't be held accountable for their actions during a hostage crisis. Their actions may result from physical or mental torture, death threats to the hostages or their families, or other forms of coercion.

Fourth, you can't have a hostage situation unless you have separation between the security warrior and the terrorist holding the hostage. If a bad guy is holding a woman with a gun or knife, you can just shoot him—this isn't considered a hostage situation because the victim is right there. If the person taken, the taker, and the warrior are in the same immediate location, it is not a hostage situation. A scenario where someone has been snatched, but the kidnapper hasn't yet gotten away calls for accurate, decisive, and aggressive action on the part of the warrior in order to prevent escalation to a hostage situation. By escalation, I mean a cessation of contact between the abductors and your team.

Last, you must have demands from the hostage taker. The demand completes the criteria for defining a hostage situation. Once these criteria have been met, it is accurate to say that you have a hostage crisis on your hands. Without a demand, there is no negotiation, and without negotiation as an option for the captives, there is only a massacre.

REASONS FOR TAKING HOSTAGES

A hostage situation can originate in one of two ways, inadvertently or deliberately. An example of an inadvertent hostage situation would be criminals who are desperate for escape after finding themselves outgunned, outnumbered, or most likely trapped during the commission of a criminal act (e.g., a robbery gone bad). A deliberate hostage crisis is one that was planned by the hostage takers from the very start. Most of the hostage crises you're likely to be familiar with were deliberate. Famous examples are the Iranian embassy siege in London in 1980, the Mumbai terrorist attacks in 2008, and the Munich massacre during the 1972 Summer Olympics. The terrorists took the hostages for one or more of the following reasons: politics, fame or recognition, money, and prisoner exchange.

Political Agenda
Often the abductors have a political agenda they want to achieve, and they think that taking hostages will assist in that. Sometimes the political objective is realized through the negotiation process.

Fame or Recognition
Fame or recognition is also a common reason for taking hostages. The group may want to publicize their cause, whether it is to make abortion illegal or to free Tibet, through a media blitz that a hostage crisis can provide. Media attention to political or social causes has motivated a number of extremists to abduct hostages.

Money
Money is the number-one motivation for criminals in hostage crises. Sometimes the hostage situations are the result of a criminal action gone wrong. Whether it is a bank robbery or a home invasion interrupted by police, the robbers take prisoners and try to negotiate their way to freedom. Sometimes the hostages were taken deliberately for the ransom. This is very common in countries where gangs or cartels operate with impunity, such as in Colombia and Mexico. It isn't difficult to determine motivations in these types of abductions.

Prisoner Exchange
Another reason for taking hostages is forcing prisoner exchanges or releases. This is frequently seen in the Middle East, such as in the case of IDF soldier Gilad Shalit, who was captured by Hamas in 2006 and was held until October 18, 2011, when he released as part

of a prisoner swap with Hamas. In exchange for Shalit's release, Israel agreed to release more than 1,000 Palestinian prisoners. Gilad was captured by Hamas on June 25, 2006, in an RPG attack on his tank. The terrorists emerged from a tunnel linked to Israel from Gaza near the Kerem Shalom border. During the attack two terrorists were killed and two IDF soldiers were killed and three were wounded. Shalit was the first soldier to be captured by enemy forces since Sergeant Nachshon Mordechai Wachsman in 1994. (Hamas kidnapped Wachsman and held him hostage for six days; he was killed during a failed rescue attempt by Israeli special forces.) Abu Shimali of Hamas was responsible for orchestrating the kidnapping of Shalit; he was killed in August 2009 in Gaza by al-Qaeda. It is common that hostage takers demand that more of their prisoners be released than the number they turn over.

Of course, there are other reasons for taking hostages, which can be personal or emotional. The ones listed here are the most common, and understanding the motivation and resolve of the terrorists or hostage takers will help the security force in its subsequent negotiations.

WHAT YOU DO

As the security agent, you need to follow a few basic steps and rules to ensure the best possible outcome for the hostages.

Confirm the Hostage Situation

Most important, you need to see the hostage situation firsthand for yourself. You can't rely on hearsay or use the reaction of others in the area to assess the real situation. You must confirm visually that there are in fact hostages being held by an armed terrorist, whose demands are stated. Only at that point can you feel confident enough to call in the cavalry (e.g., dispatch, police, fire, emergency medical services).

Your goal as the security professional on scene is to do two main things until a professional negotiation team arrives and a tactical takeover team comes into play:

1. Establish communication and then calm the hostage takers as much as possible, with words and basic negotiation tactics. For example, don't make threats or behave in an aggressive manner. Instead, try to engage them in conversation to soothe their nerves.

2. Avoid a bloody outcome for the hostages. One way to do this is to prolong the situation as long as possible. The longer the situation drags on, the better the hostages' chances to be rescued alive. As time passes, several things can happen. The terrorists may wear down and get sloppy, they may lose their edge and focus, you may be able to come to an agreement, and, most important, you have an opportunity to gather intelligence for use in a tactical takeover. This is the ultimate goal: a successful takeover with no hostage casualties. This takes time to plan and patience to wait for the opportune time.

The hostage takers don't want to die; that's why they have taken hostages in the first place. Think about the role of the hostages: they are leverage. Live hostages secure the takers' lives as negotiations continue. If the terrorists were committed to dying, they would have chosen a suicide mission or a fight to the death.

Alert Dispatch

After confirmation that a hostage situation exists, alert dispatch/management personnel of the situation, who will in turn coordinate with the local authorities. You don't want to be tied up on the phone answering questions and dealing with operators. Pass on the critical information, as defined in your communication protocol to dispatch, which will handle it from there, according to its hostage crisis protocol. Communicate only when new information becomes relevant to the situation or when dispatch asks specific questions. Initially, you must set up communication by whatever means necessary. A cell phone or radio is sufficient for getting the ball rolling. Although a more secure method of communication might be ideal, there is no time to waste. Once the hostage rescue team, negotiator, and other logistical elements are put in place, you will slowly phase out of communications.

Contain the Situation

Next, you and your security team need to contain the situation by establishing and maintaining an outer and an inner circle. Containment means not letting anyone in or out of a designated area. All individuals involved in the situation—whether hostages, terrorists, or witnesses—need to be kept for debriefing by authorities. No person not directly involved in the resolution of the situation should be permitted to enter your set perimeter, including members of the press, public onlookers, family members, or anyone else. Property owners and maintenance staff can provide a great wealth of information about the intricacies of the structure the terrorists are holed up in.

Gather Intelligence

After you have confirmed the situation, alerted the chain of command, and created a sterile area of containment, you tackle the most essential task: gathering intelligence. This will have the single greatest impact on the outcome of the situation. Vital information includes such things as the number of terrorists, the number and makeup of hostages (men, women, children; ages; physical condition), types and quantity of weapons or explosives, the interior layout of the structure (try to get blueprints if possible), the resolve of the terrorists, the nature of their demands, the time lines given, and the leadership of the group (i.e., who is the man to speak to in order to negotiate and what type of man is he—is he irrational, is he calm, do the others respect or fear him?). All this information is available through various sources: eyewitnesses, personal accounts, third party input (e.g., people familiar with the terrorists, hostages, or cause, if known), phone taps or room bugs, and security cameras, as well as various other means of gathering information.

"Knowing is half the battle" is an understatement when dealing with hostage scenarios. The importance of gathering information for use in decision making for tactical takeover teams and for negotiations cannot be overstated.

Establish Communication

Once you have established the sterile area, you need to take all necessary steps to ensure an open and clear line of communication. Communication is essential for gathering intelligence about the situation, as well as for calming the terrorists. You can establish communication in various ways: cell phone, landline, e-mail, or satellite phone. The most effective communication involves talking directly to hostage takers if possible. But no matter the means of communication, you need to keep them talking to wear them down and divulge information that may prove useful for the professional negotiator when he arrives. It is important to record everything that is communicated—sometimes small, seemingly insignificant details can be instrumental in the negotiations or the takeover.

THE NEGOTIATIONS

Once you have established a means of communication with the terrorists, it is time to start the negotiating process. As mentioned earlier, procrastination can be used to calm the terrorists as you try to negotiate the release of the hostages.

During the negotiations, you present yourself as a middleman; you don't want to be the boss because then the takers will think that you can make good on their demands, which will be out of your control or authority. You also don't want the abductors to think you're a nobody because then they will demand to speak to your superior. They have to believe that you have some decision-making power, but not the final say. This will make it seem normal when you initially negotiate for some basic demands and bargain and stall for others.

Do what you can to keep the conversation going but be careful to promise only what you can deliver. Never agree to a situation you can't handle or deliver or whose outcome you don't know. You can provide food, water, or medical supplies, but never guns, ammo, vehicles, or any other items that will enhance the abductors' bargaining position. Any type of transport vehicle (e.g., car, plane, helicopter) should be viewed as a weapon. Further, you can't give more hostages to the abductors or exchange different people for hostages or weapons. A basic rule is that you should be able to use anything you agree to give to the hostage takers to your advantage. It could be food and water laced with a sedative, communication equipment with built-in GPS, or listening equipment with a roving tap. Use their needs as a means to gather information you need. You must be savvy in how you try to get altered food or listening devices in, however. The terrorists/hostage takers will likely be suspicious of anything you send in.

Even if you have a clear shot at a terrorist and you can kill him, don't do it unless someone shoots at you first or is about to kill a hostage. Whether you succeed or fail in the attempt, the action will destroy any trust you have established, hurting your efforts for further negotiations. Plus, the abductors will punish the hostages for your actions. If you hear shooting from within or you have other evidence that the hostage takers are getting ready to kill people, then you have no choice but to storm the facility immediately. Remember that you're there only for the hostages—if not for them, you would have killed the terrorists at the first opportunity. Every security team must have a crisis-intervention capability and protocol.

MOVEMENT OF TAKERS AND HOSTAGES

The hostage takers and hostages are allowed to move from one structure to another by foot for one of the following reasons only:

there are no other people in the new structure who can be captured, or the move won't help them in any way. Ensure that there are no weapons or tools to facilitate their goals in the new structure. If possible, you need to use this move to your advantage by rigging the new location with cameras, microphones, or whatever else you can do secretly before the move is agreed upon. Just keep stalling the negotiations until a tactical takeover plan is formulated, and steps are in place for that option.

PART FIVE

DEALING WITH SUSPICIOUS PEOPLE, VEHICLES, AND OBJECTS

The golden rule for all searches is "When in doubt, check it out." The protocols of why you search, how you search, what you search, and what you're searching for are situational. Within these protocols, you must have the ability to define what is suspicious to you and your team. It's all about reading the telltale signs and signals of the situation. Nothing should go unnoticed, but some things are left up to the discretion of the warrior or checker responsible for that detail. When searching, you might come across objects that are suspicious but not necessarily dangerous. Such suspicious objects might include vehicles, electronics, weapons or bombs, and mail. And, of course, people are the most suspicious things of all.

Never forget that although a knife is a tool that cuts and a pistol is a tool that shoots, the human is the real weapon. Our concern is the person and the threats he is capable of. This means we can confirm our suspicions of the person and his intentions, but the tools alone are not sufficient for proving intent. Legally, this is known as a *false contrapositive*. If there is intent, we look for the means; if there are means, we look for an explanation. Obviously, a bomb has only one intention, but a Swiss Army knife is debatable.

Think of it like this: TSA security personnel at any airport in the United States focuses 100 percent of its attention on your belongings and almost none on *you*. But if they find a knife in your bag, they will act as if there is intent by *you* to do harm. What they *should* do first is analyze whether *you* are a threat and then determine whether there is a means to confirm this suspicion. Or they may determine that the knife was mistakenly placed in the bag.

CHAPTER 20

Suspicious People

Suspicious people can generally be categorized by their actions, their appearance, or their belongings. As stated before, everybody who attempts to enter your secured facility or interact with your protected party, no matter who they are, must be checked on some level to determine the threat level to your client. Be alert for any signs that telegraph that a person is a greater threat to your client when you first encounter him. If someone does exhibit red flags, you automatically scrutinize him more thoroughly.

RED FLAGS

What are some of the red flags that make an individual suspicious and worthy of further scrutiny? The list is endless, but the following are the most common warnings that should set off your security antenna.

The first sign is inappropriate clothing, such as a winter coat being worn in the heat of the summer or a man wearing a suit when everyone else is in casual attire. Bizarre or unsuitable clothing is often the most obvious tell that the person may be a security threat.

The next sign consists of behavioral characteristics, including but not limited to the following:

- **Fidgeting.** This could include nervous movement of the hands or feet. Keep your eyes on this person and engage him.

- **Sweating excessively for the situation.** For example, you should keep your eye on anyone sweating profusely even though the temperature is not hot enough and his activity is not strenuous enough to produce that much perspiration. Nervous tension makes people sweat.

- **Refusing to make eye contact.** This is a telltale behavioral sign in people who are ashamed of their actions or are afraid of attracting attention to themselves.

- **Pacing frenetically.** This is common in people too amped up to calm down. This is a typical sign that something is about to happen.

- **Repeatedly looking at a watch or cell phone.** This could indicate that the person is nervously waiting for a certain time or signal to act.

- **Communicating secretly with another person in the area.** This could help you identify two terrorists planning an act of violence. In the case of a suicide bombing, this might mean that one terrorist has the actual bomb on his person and the other is there to remotely detonate the bomb if the first person is reluctant to set it off or is caught by the authorities.

- **Appearing to be in a trance.** Anyone who is walking around or sitting in an apparent daze could be so brainwashed to carry out his mission that he is no longer able to engage in normal dialogue or respond to any type of interaction. Keep your eyes on a person displaying this behavior.

The final indication of a suspicious person is the presence of inappropriate belongings, such as a suitcase at a park, a large electronic device in a movie theater, or a child's backpack on an adult who is unaccompanied by a child. Terrorists often choose to leave a child's backpack in a public place because it appears more innocent (it is easier to imagine a child leaving his pack in a public place than an adult forgetting his). Seeing the child's pack on an adult is more suspicious than finding it in an inappropriate setting because the bag might have actually been left inadvertently; of course, you still must investigate any bag left unattended in a public place.

If you encounter a suspicious person, it is important to survey the scene thoroughly and think outside the box. Try to enter the mind of the attacker and think like a person who is planning an attack on your facility or client. If you see a male coming out of the women's bathroom, this is suspicious from a security perspective, so find out why he was in the wrong rest room.

When searching a suspicious individual, do it in a separate area that is out of sight of the public. Do this so that other terrorists who are nearby watching do not see specifically what you are looking for and how you physically search suspicious individuals or their belongings. Also the search does not distract the other security warriors from observing other individuals who also warrant attention. It also puts greater pressure on the party being searched, almost forcing him to act, in which case the warriors are present during the search to deal with it.

The area where the searches are conducted must be safe and secure. Ideally, a professional checker performs the search, while a security warrior tasked with protecting him stands by to take action if needed. Search the suspicious person first and then his belongings. It depends on what you're looking for, but an airport-style magnetic gate or a metal detector may be sufficient. In more sensitive cases, you may need the person to remove his shoes, jacket, belt, hat, and watch, and to empty his pockets so that you can check every item individually. Always know what you're looking for in advance.

As discussed earlier, checking is a separate function and should be performed by a specific individual who has been specifically trained in questioning, searching, and using specialized equipment. Checkers are usually experts in spotting fake IDs, lies, and hidden weapons and compartments. Security warriors don't conduct the search unless it is an emergency, such as a suspected suicide bomber or an armed individual. Searching isn't your profession and would distract you from your combat duties. But you should know how to do it just in case you are needed.

As a warrior you must always back up the checkers 100 percent with whatever they ask. They are the brains and know their job; you are the muscle, and you know yours. Typically, checkers are young women, and this is important because they can check both sexes, and it is easier for women to talk to both sexes. It is not uncommon for a man to let his guard down when a young woman is asking to see his ID and asking questions about him. These women are trained to be shrewd, cunning, and smartly focused. They will be able to see right through things that are a facade.

CHAPTER 21

Suspicious Vehicles

Although vehicles are objects, I have chosen to treat them separately because their ability to harm is so great. Other suspicious objects are covered in the next chapter.

Just as we discussed what it means to search a person and identify any suspicious signs, it is equally important to be able to identify all the indicators of a suspicious vehicle.

Most of us see lots of vehicles every day. Other than clogging the streets, polluting the air, and occasionally running into each other, they seem pretty innocuous. But vehicles can easily be modified to use as weapons or to transport the enemy. To stop a vehicular attack, you must first identify the threat so that you can attack preemptively. Remember, action is always faster and more effective at stopping a threat than reaction.

The most obvious indicator of a suspicious vehicle is a suspect action. A vehicle repeatedly circling a block or driving erratically can be a red flag that the vehicle may be dangerous to your client. More specific red flags include the following:

- Front and rear license plates don't match.
- Door locks look tampered with or damaged.
- Signs that the interior electronics, dashboard, or ignition

have been tampered with (could indicate that the vehicle was stolen for the attack).

- Vehicle with extreme weight on one side or in the rear.
- Abandoned car in a no-parking or no-standing zone (might indicate that it is being used for illegal activity or as a bomb).
- Bumper stickers with political messages that appear to have been placed haphazardly, perhaps to look the part and fit in.
- Tinted or covered windows that prohibit you from seeing inside the vehicle.
- Commercial vehicles without signs on them.
- Terrorists often use older government cars when targeting public buildings or spaces (for example, a federal court-house or an airport) because they blend in with the official vehicles in the surrounding area. Civilians often mistake the vehicles as undercover police cars, and they might even fool a trained eye at a quick glance.

If a vehicle's driver or passenger looks or acts suspicious, then you must consider the vehicle itself as suspect. It has to be thoroughly inspected, along with its occupants. Again, in security work, it

The extreme weight in the rear of this car makes it suspicious. You should stop it and check both its occupants and its contents carefully before allowing it to approach your facility. If the occupants of this vehicle seem suspicious, cuff and search them, and call in a bomb squad, bomb dog, or robot.

is better to be safe than sorry, especially when considering the destructive potential a vehicle has when used as a weapon. All vehicle searches should be conducted at a designated area dedicated to that purpose, if possible.

Search the passengers before you inspect the vehicle. First, check their documentation and identification and then take the passengers to a separate area and each is searched. The intensity of the search has a lot to do with "what am I interested in finding?" If it is a pistol or a razor blade, this dictates how thorough you must be. Complete the searches of the people before you inspect their belongings; that way they cannot pull out a weapon while you are looking through their bags.

Ideally, the first security barrier is a metal detector gate, like at the airport, to establish that security is important and all individuals are considered suspicious. The magnetic gate will pick up any large objects, such as firearms, bombs, and knives. If the gate indicates nothing suspicious, then you use the wand before allowing individuals to pass. Pass the wand over every surface of the body closely, making contact and overlapping with each pass.

If the gate indicates the presence of something suspicious, you must conduct a more thorough physical search, including cavity searches. If possible, females should search females, and males search males. Ask the person to stand like a starfish, with arms held out to the sides and the feet wide apart. For a hand search, place your hands together, thumb to thumb, and pass them over every inch of the body, including the hair, armpit, crotch, waistline, and feet.

For wanding or pat-downs, people are required to remove coats, belts, hats, shoes, wallets, phones, watches, and jewelry. Some common hiding places for weapons are in shoes, behind watches, behind belt buckles, at the waistline, in underwear, under hats or inside hatbands, in the hair, behind cell phone batteries (a razor blade fits nicely here), in wallets, and, of course, in bags, cases, and boxes. While the checker inspects the people, the warrior stands behind and protects her so that she can do her job thoroughly. We use women because they are automatically good cops, in the "good cop/bad cop game" we play with suspicious parties.

Next, the vehicle is checked meticulously for any irregularities, weapons, or explosives. As when searching an interior structure, with a vehicle you start from the bottom and work up, covering three levels. First, inspect the undercarriage, including the wheel wells and under the bumpers. Next, tackle the interior of the vehicle, including the passenger compartment, center console, floor mats, glove box, trunk, spare-tire compartment, battery area, and under the hood. Finally, look on the roof of the vehicle, especially on large trucks, checking out any storage containers, luggage or sports equipment racks, or any other attachments. Use a good flashlight when inspecting dark spaces. If you have trained bomb-sniffing dogs available, use one. Dogs don't get complacent, and can act without prejudice or emotion.

To do a thorough investigation of a vehicle, you must have a basic understanding of the engine's parts and bay, as well as what the underneath of a truck's frame should look like. Inspectors need to be aware of the threat of remote detonation. If the car is searched in the same location that it is initially stopped, it could be remote-detonated, thereby killing other innocents in the vicinity. Explosives have been found hidden in the headlight assembly, bumpers, wheel wells, behind the dashboard, and in the frame of a large commercial truck. This is why trained checkers equipped with mirrors, flashlights, and other more specific equipment should conduct the search if possible. The inspection is conducted while the driver and passengers are kept at a safe distance under the watchful eye of the security warrior. Use dogs if available to search for explosives.

CHAPTER 22

Suspicious Objects

If you encounter a suspicious object, you need to know exactly what to do. A set protocol is needed for dealing with any unidentified, suspicious, or unclaimed object that could be harmful. As soon as you arrive on scene and spot a suspicious object or have one reported to you, you must react immediately. The following actions are recommended:

1. Get the attention of people in the general vicinity and ask loudly whether anyone wishes to claim the object.

2. If there is no immediate response, then you must inspect the bag visually and externally for any suspicious signs.

3. Assess its threat level immediately to decide if you open up a sterile area around the object (the safest option) or drop it in a "bomb hole" if the bag seems safe. A bomb hole is a deep concrete and steel well, located outside public facilities for disposing of suspicious items.

4. Clear everyone as far away as possible, and don't let anyone get close—and that includes you. After that, contact dispatch to

explain that you have a potentially explosive object and request a bomb-disposal unit.

5. Search the perimeter or the exterior of the building at different levels of intensity based on distance from the building: 5, 25, and 50 meters. Each distance requires a different intensity of search because the degree of danger increases the closer the object is to the structure. When searching a perimeter (or internal area, for that matter), the amount of time you'll need is determined by two factors: the size of the suspected object and the size of the area to be searched. Realistically, finding a scalpel in a movie theater isn't reasonable, but finding a .22-caliber pistol there would be.

The first level of the exterior search is within 5 meters of the structure's outer wall or gate. At this level, you're searching for any object that resembles a hand grenade in shape or size. An object of this size could damage the outer walls, but an object smaller than this can't break down the outer walls at 5 meters.

The second search level takes place 25 meters from the exterior walls. At this distance, the search focuses on objects the size of a shoe box or larger, which can cause damage to the facility's structure.

The third level takes place at 50 meters or more. At this distance, it is important to search for all items that seem out of place in the designated area. An individual sitting in a parked car with its motor running across the street from a protected house is suspicious and worth checking out. A newspaper box or mailbox that is new to the area is another example of a potential threat that you have to investigate to make sure it is harmless.

6. In addition to the above perimeter searches for objects, you must also conduct another search for suspicious individuals who may be moving in and out of your comfort zone. These individuals need to be watched, monitored, checked for identities, and/or interviewed based on the situation. This determination is based on the judgment of the security staff.

Suspicious Objects

For the purposes of this section, I have selected the most common suspicious objects that you as a security warrior will encounter: weapons, electronics, bombs, and mail.

WEAPONS

"Hot" items and "cold" items can be used to categorize some of the weapons looked for during any type of search (e.g., a person, perimeter, interior, or vehicle). Hot-item weapons are those that use combustion and are known for their range. Some examples are a pistol, rifle, automobile, airplane, bomb, and grenade, or could even be a combination of hair spray and a lighter. Cold weapons have a more limited range. Examples of cold weapons include a brick, hammer, knife, ax, and anything else that could be used in a violent way. A cold weapon won't go empty or jam, so it is always operational.

Within these two types of weapons categories, you have three ranges of weapons: near, medium, and far. Near-range weapons are those that can be used at an arm's length, such as a pistol, hammer, bomb, and machete, all of which can be concealed and used at arm's length and immediate distances. Medium-range weapons include items that can be used at more than an arm's length distance but are still in plain view, such as a rifle, pistol, or hand grenade. Far-range weapons are those that may be out of sight completely. Examples include sniper rifle, airplane, and rocket-propelled grenade.

Being able to categorize the weapons into types (hot or cold) and ranges (near, medium, far) will help you plan your procedures for countering or defending an attack. It will also make search protocols easier to develop for your security situation and needs.

ELECTRONICS

Electronic objects are broken down into two categories: those that can be used to conceal a weapon and still perform their electrical function, and those that can't still function once modified to hold a weapon.

When judging whether an electronic device should be searched, you must consider what type of weapon you're looking for. For example, if you're searching for something as small as a razor blade, you must think outside the box to ensure safety. Searching behind the battery in a cell phone would be justified because a razor blade could be concealed there, which could be a threat to you and your client if undiscovered. On the other hand, if you're searching for a pistol, taking a battery out of a cell phone has zero relevance. Another example would be taking the back off a television or a speaker box to search for a weapon the size of a hand grenade. The most important thing to realize when searching electronic objects is that the cell phone, speaker, and TV can all function normally with a potentially harmful object inside them. That is why you may have to disassemble them, at least partially, to ensure safety. You can't just have the owner operate the device (e.g., make a call on the cell phone) and assume it isn't being used to smuggle in a weapon.

The second type of suspicious electronic device is one that can't function with a weapon inside. In October 1998 the Israeli Ministry of Defense uncovered a Hamas cell that had been training its members in the use of explosives and detonation devices, with remote detonation and suspension detonation as their specialty. In particular, they planted the devices inside videocassette tapes. Mouhi Aldin Alsharif was the explosives expert for the Hamas wing working out of Jerusalem. He had booby-trapped several videotapes to explode by remote detonation. The primary explosive used was a chemical substance called TATP. There were 11 rigged cassette tapes set to be placed in phone booths and parks in Petah Tikva, Israel. Fortunately, only one tape exploded in a video store in Natania, moderately injuring a customer. In the end the whole cell was uncovered, and five of the cell members were arrested and imprisoned for terms ranging from 9 to 24 years.

This is the basic procedure to follow when searching large electronic objects. Again, your objective is to create a balance of what is secure and what is reasonable for a given situation. It will vary greatly.

BOMBS

You must do a thorough search for explosives when you arrive at a new location, or when you search perimeters, vehicles, and persons and their belongings. Explosives can come in a variety of forms and strengths, so you need a basic understanding of them in order to know what to look for and how to describe them when reporting the bomb. To begin with, all bombs must have three parts to work properly: the explosive itself (e.g., dynamite, C-4, muriatic acid and tin foil), an ignition system (e.g., fire or electricity source), and a timer (e.g., a wick, clock, cigarette, or any other part that controls the ignition system or the substances' ability to work together).

In the past, bombs have been hidden in just about anything you can think of, including a watermelon, beer can, cell phone, backpack, and hot pot. When the bomb explodes, it will expel heat, sound, fire, a shock wave, and shrapnel, which produce various types and degrees of damage. For example, a blast contained in, say, a lobby will be deadlier than the same blast in an open field. This is analogous to a firecracker going off on your arm as opposed to in your hand—in the former, you get burned; in the latter, you lose your fingers.

Explosives can be categorized into two main categories: homemade and factory manufactured. Homemade bombs are generally less effective and harder to use, but they are easier to come by. Factory-produced bombs are, on the other hand, generally more effective and easier to use but harder to obtain.

You may encounter several types of explosive material in the field, and a checker must be familiar with all of them in order to spot and identify them quickly and accurately. Below I have listed some of the most common forms, along with selected characteristics.

- TNT can be molded into several shapes and be made to look like harmless items, such as a plate or a garden gnome. TNT can be painted and is therefore very difficult to detect when placed among other common items.

- Detasheet is a flat, rubber-like explosive made of PETN, nitrocellulose, and a binder. It can be any color and can be made into a lot of flexible materials, such as upholstery or clothing. It is detonated with a cord or blasting cap.
- Detonating cord (also called det cord or detacord) is used to detonate other explosives, such as C-4, and can be woven into other fabric objects, such as a suitcase or coat. Det cord weighs 12 grams per meter.
- C-4 is a variant of the plastic explosive Composition C. C-4 is a moldable, gray Play-Doh–like substance that comes in brick form. It is extremely powerful and commonly used in the military. It consists primarily of an explosive element (usually RDX), a binder to make it more stable and less sensitive to shock and heat, and a plasticizer to make it malleable. It is detonated with a blasting cap.
- Nitrocellulose is a cotton-like (it is sometimes referred to as *guncotton*), extremely powerful explosive, but it must be tightly contained in order to explode. It is produced by nitrating cellulose and has been around since the 1840s.
- EDGN (ethylene glycol dinitrate) is a jelly-like explosive substance that can be any color and is without scent. It is often an ingredient in dynamite and nitroglycerin.
- Nitroglycerin looks like water, has no smell or taste, and is extremely powerful. It is obtained by nitrating glycerol. It has been used since the mid-19th century, especially in dynamite, but it is very unstable. It was heavily used in both World War I and II. Nitroglycerin weighs 1.7 kilos per liter, so it is identifiable from water by its weight (H_2O is 1 liter per kilo).

The above list is far from complete. New explosives are developed all the time, and it is difficult to keep up with the newest methods and technology being used by terror organizations. The use of explosives (for example, for breaching or search-and-rescue purposes) and their disposal (explosive ordnance disposal, or EOD) are separate professions within security and should be respected as such. Very specialized training is required for their team members.

The case of Anne Marie Murphy is a great example of how specially trained security agents thwarted an attempt to smuggle a bomb onboard an airplane. On Thursday, April 17, 1986, at London's Heathrow International Airport, a plot was uncovered to blow up an El Al Airline Boeing 747 plane midflight with a timer-detonated suitcase bomb. The suitcase belonged to Anne Marie Murphy, a 32-year-old Irish woman, who was six months pregnant. Murphy was completely unremarkable and did not show any suspicious signs to security staff when questioned. Her checked bag did, however, raise some serious red flags. First, her bag was strangely heavy for its size and contents. Next, a look inside revealed a scientific calculator with electrical cables protruding from it. Soon after that bag search, the bomb was found. It had a timing device, Semtex as the detonator, and a large cache of explosives set to explode midflight.

Murphy was arrested but never charged after an investigation revealed that she had no knowledge of the explosive device. Nizar Hindawi, a Jordanian working with the Syrian intelligence service, had given the bag to her and planted the explosive device in it and rigged it to go off. Hindawi had seduced Murphy, impregnated her, and later married her as part of a plot to use her as a mule for the bomb. The Syrians alerted Hindawi of Murphy's arrest at the airport and harbored him in the Syrian embassy and a Syrian safe house. British police later arrested him, and on October 25, 1986, Hindawi was convicted for his part in the attempted bomb plot and sentenced to 45 years in prison.

This example shows how good security measures and well-trained staff uncovered and prevented a terrorist plot that would have resulted in the death of hundreds. By following a simple search protocol of Murphy's bag, airline agents discovered the bomb. Note that despite the fact that Murphy raised no red flags in her initial interview, her bags were still checked thoroughly, during which the calculator was found, which led to the discovery of the bomb.

MAIL

Remember the golden rule for all searches? *When in doubt, check it out.* This rule applies to mail as well. Checkers must scrutinize letters and packages that arrive in the secured facility to make sure they have no irregularities that make them suspicious.

The following should alert you that a package or letter might be dangerous:

- Too many stamps, which could signal that the sender wanted to ensure that the piece wouldn't be returned
- A piece of mail with no return address or incorrect or misspelled titles or names
- Different cities in the postmark and the return address
- Any package that is extremely heavy for its size, smells strange, or has discolorations or an oily stain
- Any package or piece of mail that arrives by unconventional means, at an irregular time, or by an unknown carrier, or one that just appears mysteriously
- Mail that has no stamps or uncancelled stamps
- A returned piece that you did not send in the first place
- Packages with protruding wires, exposed tinfoil, or a ticking sound may indicate a bomb.
- Packages with too much tape
- Any letter or package marked "Personal" or "Confidential" or "To be opened only by [specific person]"

It is important to consider all possibilities when controlling what is let into the sterile area. Mail can be X-rayed, weighed, and swabbed for explosive material. But as with all other searches, the level of scrutiny depends on the level and type of threat you're defending against. For example, if you provide protection for a businessman while he moves diamonds, gold, or cash through the city, you should be more concerned about an ambush than a letter bomb. On the other hand, if your client is a political figure, you must pay close attention to incoming mail because of the high-profile nature of the client.

PART SIX
MOBILE SECURITY

With mobile security work, you must be ready to act on a moment's notice, and you must be sharp and accurate at all times—no matter where you are. One major difference between providing security on the move and at a static location is that with the former you're always in potential enemy territory, and you have to be dynamic. You need to understand that your responsibility is greater when not in your home court, and failure will likely have much graver consequences when you're on the move.

But in real life, security work often involves travel, so you need to plan and train for any mobile security you might be expected to provide. Sometimes your travel will take you to other countries, which have their own laws regarding security personnel. You have to be knowledgeable about these laws and how they impact your operations. For example, many nations won't allow foreign security forces to carry weapons within their borders; some nations even prohibit their own citizens from owning or using weapons. This can make you and your client extremely vulnerable, especially in places like the United Kingdom, where knife attacks are regular and guns are forbidden. You need a plan of action before you leave home.

If you're traveling to an allied Western country on a government-sanctioned dignitary-protection detail, your diplomatic status might give you immunity from search and prosecution, thereby allowing you to carry a sidearm. Again the particulars will be nation-specific and must be nailed down before you depart. If you're protecting a business guest of the local government, you might not be permitted to bring weapons into the country, but you might be facilitated in acquiring the weapons once you arrive in country and allowed to carry them during your stay.

If you're working in a country where foreigners are strictly forbidden from possessing weapons and being caught with them could result in heavy jail sentences, the best thing is to contact the local law enforcement authorities in advance and hire off-duty officers to provide armed escort and an outer security perimeter. Your team will still maintain the inner circle to the best of your restricted abilities, but you should find some trusted local contacts to work with. The biggest problem here, of course, will be finding local personnel who are trustworthy. But, again, each situation and country will pose separate threats and security challenges.

It is possible to get a U.S. State Department permit to travel internationally with firearms. With the permit, you may take a maximum of three guns and 1,000 rounds of ammo per man. The trick is not *getting* the permit, which I have; the trick is *using* it. You see, in order to use the permit you must get permission from the country you are flying into to have a firearm on your person. Depending on where you are going, this can be difficult or even impossible. I have found both. But I have also found two loopholes in this system for some countries. The first one works great in Africa. I was working closely with a transport security company that was escorting gold dust throughout Africa and to a refinery in Miami over the better part of 2010. We realized that we could legally get a hunting permit in most countries in Africa. With such a permit, we could cheaply acquire rifles and have them on our persons and in our cars. Hunting rifles are not ideal weapons for security work, but you may not have your Glock and AR, and you will at least have firepower. I have used this tactic on more then one occasion without issue.

The second loophole I found was when I was working closely

A maritime security team training on floating targets at sea. A sniper team is one of the best defenses you can have against pirates.

with a maritime security team off the Horn of Africa in 2011. You can have any weapon you please in international waters for counter-piracy operations. The trick is keeping the weapons in international waters. What we had to do was have a ship that would always be staging off the coast and wait until it could rendezvous with the freighter for its voyage. This can get complicated if you want to follow the rules, but it can work smoothly if you have solid contracts with shippers and enough manpower.

Of course, mobile security extends beyond firearms. This section details the most common means of travel and the dangers inherent in each. Each mobile security detail, like every security installation, has its weak points. For example, while an airport doesn't permit scissors and pocketknives, it does allow glass bottles. As any true warrior knows, broken glass in trained hands can be more intimidating and devastating than a pocketknife. Likewise, every mode of travel has weaknesses, and it is particularly important that each member of the security team understands what the weak points in their itinerary are and when they are most vulnerable. The team needs to assess from the perspective of the enemy where these weaknesses are. Just as each warrior should take time to learn the weaknesses of his facility by conducting a half-day recon mission, each man must analyze the various legs of an upcoming trip to comprehend the weak points and therefore prepare to better defend against them. All possible threats, both unique to the specific detail and general to your journey, need to be discussed so that a specific plan for reduction, prevention, or reaction can be created for them. Several threats will have similar solutions, but all threats need to be planned for, big and small.

The best thing is a group brainstorming session to talk about what-ifs and Murphy's law.

CHAPTER 23

Travel by Private Vehicle

As a security warrior, you will probably travel more by private vehicle than any other means of transportation. Even if part of the trip is by plane, chances are an automobile ride will be on your itinerary as well. For example, getting to or from the airport might include a ride in a cab, limousine, or rental car.

The primary rule involving travel by private vehicle is that you get the vehicle as close as possible to the structure where the passengers are waiting to load or unload. This allows you to load or unload them quickly and minimize that window of vulnerability. That's the most vulnerable moment for you and your client: when moving from one closed sterile area to another.

Driving forward in a vehicle is always safer than going in reverse, so always back into parking spaces if you can. This speeds up hasty departures and also gives the driver a more useful field of view. When you're working in a two-vehicle convoy (with VIPs in each one), each vehicle must work independently in an emergency, so your driver must be your friend as well as a lookout so you can trust him to be alert to threats.

Use the same driver and vehicle for the duration of the trip. Remember, a driver doesn't have to be trained as a security warrior, but he should be armed with a pistol and know how to shoot defensively. While working, he must be focused on his duties as the driver, and that's it. As a professional driver, he should be the master of his vehicle's dynamics, whether it is a BMW M5 or a bus. Vehicles should be "sleepers": low-key machines that are prepped for performance.

You should be able to ram with your vehicle, take sharp turns at high speeds, execute emergency lane changes, and control skids on wet or loose pavement. Fast acceleration is essential for passing and outrunning threats. Remember, speed is protection. In bodyguard work, it is better to have a nimble and agile machine with less armor than to have a slow, heavy tank. Depending on your environment, you need to decide what is more important, armor or agility, much like the gear you carry on your person. (For more information on tactical driving, see Chapter 11.)

Some security personnel present themselves overtly with M4 rifles and bulletproof vests, while others operate covertly in civilian clothes with concealed or discreet handguns and cell phones for communication. For example, if you're working undercover with a traveling group, you want to blend in with the others in your party, as should your vehicles. On the other hand, if you're working in Africa, the Middle East, or South America, you might be better off looking the part with military-type gear.

The vehicle's motor should always be left running, and an automatic transmission is best for security work. The car can idle for loading and unloading, without putting it in park, by just holding the

A military-like presence can make your overland travel much safer in certain regions of the world.

hand brake momentarily. Newer cars do this with the touch of a button, usually called "hold." This is because acceleration is faster when you mash on the gas, overriding the parking brake and lowering it after the initial surge of acceleration and movement. The park mode requires you to push the brake, shift, and then accelerate. The best setup I have seen is the SMG transmission of the BMW M-series cars, which allows you to idle without rolling. The car automatically will hold an auto-slipper clutch, which engages when you push on the gas. The driver secures the vehicle when you get out with the passengers. You are first out and last in. Don't hold the door—you're not a butler. Be alert and focus on the area of greatest threat, such as a crowd of people, a van with blacked-out windows, or a dark alley. Always keep the windows up and doors locked.

Both you and the driver should search the vehicle (he knows the vehicle best) before you start the trip, and ideally it should never be left unattended thereafter. The driver remains with the vehicle at all times. If a vehicle must be left standing unattended for a long period, such as in a parking lot or garage, it must be searched thoroughly before it is re-entered. This search is for any sort of tampering, including bombs or tracking devices. Searching a car thoroughly for signs of tampering takes two men about 15 minutes. It is best to use dogs to sniff out the bombs in all cases where an explosive device is a real possibility. A good precaution is to have riveted skid-type plates installed under the car to prevent the planting of tracking or explosive devices. The riveting will also make the vehicle search much easier. The ignition-mounted bomb is the most common type of vehicle bomb and the easiest to install. A smart counter to this is to equip your vehicle with remote-start capability. If you suspect such a bomb, you can start the car from a safe distance before security and VIPs are even close.

Under ideal conditions, the vehicle is monitored by cameras, motion detectors, and security guards, or locked in a secured garage. In some cases, especially while you're away from your secure facility, this is impossible. An old trick is to sprinkle talcum powder around

When traveling by vehicle, you should have a security team consisting of a driver and security warrior at the very least. More security warriors are needed for certain situations.

the car and to check for footprints when you return. Israelis use finely combed dirt around the security fences in the West Bank and Gaza.

When preparing for the trip, make the driver part of the route planning and ensure that he is familiar with all alternate routes. All the primary and alternate routes need to be predetermined and secured before the journey, as well as what signs must be present to justify an alternate route. You must know the location of the closest police station to your destination, as well as all stations along the route. This is useful information in case you're followed or pursued. Driving to a police station would obviously deter would-be attackers, and the cameras in and around the police compound could be useful in the identification or apprehension of the pursuers.

The security team needs to know the fastest routes to all hospitals along your route and close to your eventual destination. This is invaluable information when someone in your group needs medical attention. All the warriors need to know combat first aid and have a basic medical kit they can use while en route to the hospital. It is faster and more secure for you as the responsible security warrior to drive a wounded person to the hospital as soon as the combat is over. That is why you memorized hospital locations and routes before

Every member of your team should know all the routes to and from your destination, as well as all alternate routes in case of detours. These routes should be marked on maps available to the team in case you have to improvise.

This is a typical vehicle for security forces in the Middle East.

leaving for the trip. The security team should drill all emergency procedures together and work with the same protocols.

When doing executive/VIP protection details, your vehicles need to be in tiptop shape. Just like you clean and inspect your weapon after firing, and make sure your communication equipment has new or recharged batteries at all times, you must do an extensive vehicle examination before beginning your journey. You start on the exterior of the vehicle and then move under the hood and on to the interior. The following checklist of things your should examine will help.

- Tires, air pressure, and lug nuts if travel is off-road

- Exterior lights, including bright, brake, and hazard lights
- Coolant, oil, washer fluid, and all other fluid levels
- Door locks (always keep them locked)
- Horn
- Air conditioning or heating
- Brakes
- Gas tank (fill up the day before the trip if you can)
- Window switches
- Interior lights and electricity, as well as any other items specific to your vehicle
- Gear/supplies: fix-a-flat, first aid kit, fire extinguisher, jumper cables, basic tools, one gallon of water per person, snacks, flashlight, and communications equipment
- Additional firepower, such as a Mossberg 590 shotgun or an M4-type rifle with a Trijicon X4 ACOG

Both the driver sand you should know where all the special equipment is and how to use it: fire extinguisher, glass hammer, fire blanket, first aid kit, and repair gear.

If attacked in transit, each vehicle containing a VIP is autonomous. The response to an attack should be as follows:

1. Fire at the attackers/other vehicles containing VIPs break off.
2. Scream, "Get down!"
3. Accelerate and don't slow down or stop until you get to a nearby police station or other designated safe area.

Remember, your most vulnerable points in the journey are when you're leaving the first location and when you're arriving at the final destination, even if you vary your routes. The starting and ending parts of your journey are always the same, so those are two places your attackers will know you're most vulnerable. That is why you have to take extra precautions during these two times, and it is also why you should never divulge schedules or destinations if you can prevent it.

Travel by Private Vehicle

When traveling on unsecured highways in hostile areas, you need adequate mobile force protection.

Traveling in a vehicle always has a risk of an ambush, so you must have a specific drill for countering different types of ambushes along the route. Ramming your way out is usually the best option, but some scenarios may require you to stay and fight it out. It is essential to train for a counterambush and have sound tactics particular to your vehicle, environment, manpower, and firepower. For example, think about how you might handle an attack by a gang in Somalia in a four-door truck with rifles and a four-man team. That response would be very different than when dealing with an attack by criminals in Liberty City, Miami, when you're one guard armed with only a pistol in an armored S-Class Mercedes.

If you don't have enough staff for a dedicated driver, you should hire a local off-duty police officer. This is especially useful when working in a foreign country. The cop will know the local routes and how to get around in his city. Besides being a great source of local intelligence, he will also be a great liaison to law enforcement, if that proves necessary. He will be legally armed and have basic firearms training, marksmanship skills, and the right mindset, all of which give him an advantage over a simple chauffeur. Most important, police officers spend plenty of time behind the wheel of a heavy sedan in all sorts of situations, and this experience will prove to be very useful in performing the driving duties of your detail. Of course, you should check out the officer's background to make sure he is trustworthy and not related to any of your client's known adversaries.

CHAPTER 24

Travel by Public Transport

If you're traveling by public means—such as a commercial airliner, ship, or train—it is best to be low key. You want to blend in so you don't attract opportunistic criminals or tip off enemies. Don't alert staff unnecessarily or draw any sort of attention to your VIPs or to yourself as the security element.

"Loose lips sink ships," so keep quiet about plans and itineraries. This advice is worth reiterating today with all the social networking venues. Make sure that your client (or anyone on your security detail) doesn't post travel plans on Facebook or Twitter. This may be more of a possibility if the travel party has teens or young adults who routinely use texting, e-mailing, or social networking sites. You never know who's listening to such "talk," and you don't want to inadvertently give out any information that assassins or terrorists could use to plan an attack. No one should know what weapons you have, the size of your security detail, where you're going or coming from, or what resources you have. This might seem obvious, but, again, keep quiet at all costs.

AIR

If possible, you should use a private jet and airfield. This is a far superior way to travel from a security perspective. To begin with, *you and only you* will be responsible for the security of your VIP. You can drive your car right up to the aircraft; personally control who is on the airfield and the plane; do any preliminary scouting, searching, and screening you wish; and carry weapons on the aircraft (but not necessarily off the aircraft at your destination). You know the pilot and crew, and you have all baggage in your custody at all times. The advantages to this mode of travel are obvious and innumerable.

When you travel on public airlines and use public airports, at least in the United States, you cede a lot of control to the incompetent Transportation and Security Agency (TSA), and there isn't much you can do about it. In the United States, you can store your weapons in your checked bags, but you must declare them at the ticket counter. Trusting Department of Homeland Security and TSA personnel to provide security in the airport, on the plane, and for your baggage is a big risk.

Given my background in the IDF, I may be biased here, but Israeli airline security is the best in the world. The Ben Gurion International Airport outside Tel Aviv is the most secure public place on the planet, and it pioneered the air marshal program (Israeli air marshals aren't ex-cops, but rather former IDF combat veterans). The same can't be said about the safety of U.S. air carriers and airports. I would encourage anyone who is a carrier bodyguard or executive protection operative to simply visit Israel and see what it is like from the time you pull onto the airport's property until you board the plane. I promise you won't feel safer anywhere else. The reason is simple: airport security agencies have invested heavily in their personnel, both in their selection and training. According to *USA Today,* the United States spends $8 per passenger for screening and security purposes, while Israel spends $50 per passenger.

It is best to not check your bags, but if you're carrying weapons, you must. Before you're separated from your bags, count how many bags there are, mark them for easy recognition, and lock them to make tampering more difficult (if traveling in the United States, you might want to use TSA-approved locks, which can be opened with a

Travel by Public Transport

This security agent is traveling by air with a rifle in his bag. Of course, before the bag is checked, the agent must declare that it contains a firearm. Make sure you know the laws of the country, state, and city before arriving at any airport with a firearm, and that you conform to them.

master key, to avoid damage to the bags themselves). Baggage that leaves your control at any point needs to be accounted for when you get it back. If possible, use dogs to sniff for explosives. If dogs are unavailable, X-ray machines or a special paper that can be rubbed on the surface of a bag can be used to check for explosive materials. Failing those measures, simply open and feel each bag for anomalies before returning them to the VIP.

SHIP

If you're traveling on your own ship, then there are several factors you need to consider, namely treating the ship as a moving installation to protect. You need at least two security warriors topside 24/7 to watch the water in all directions for threats. The security warriors need to be armed with long weapons, at least an M4 rifle with a Trijicon ACOG scope, to protect the ship from a distance. They also need powerful searchlights and night-vision scopes on the rifles.

Like with the roving vehicle convoy, a chase boat is also a good idea as an escape or rescue craft. This boat, manned with security personnel, will also act as the outer circle and first line of defense. The equipment and principles needed to secure the ship are quite similar to those for a static installation, as stated above, with the addition of maritime safety equipment as needed by any sizable vessel. As when protecting a land facility, the crew and captain need to be checked and briefed, and must work smoothly with security to provide the best balance of security while infringing on the lifestyle of the protected personnel as little as possible.

The best defense against pirates is deterrence. Pirates are opportunistic criminals, meaning they want the easy job. You can minimize your vulnerability by making your ship seem less of a sure thing. A following boat is best for outer-perimeter defense, as it can intercept pirate boats posing as fishing vessels. Modern pirates are using a mother ship to launch multiple fishing skiffs to attack at once. The watch team must observe from a fortified high point on the ship, primarily with one man watching port and aft and one watching starboard and aft. The captain will naturally be watching straight ahead, but pirates attack and board moving ships from the sides and tie up at the rear for stability. This is what has happened in the past.

Once the security team spots a potential threat, one team member follows it with a spotting scope or binoculars, while the other immediately gets the ship in the sights of his rifle scope. Both men continue to scrutinize the vessel to determine whether it is a pirate ship; if it is, then the captain is alerted. This puts several things into action. First, the other two security warriors are summoned to the deck. Next, the crew members gather in the safe room. Finally, the captain alerts the relevant authorities.

The best type of rifle for this kind of work is the SR-25 7.62mm sniper system. A tripod, a bench, or at the very least a bipod is necessary. Rifles should be kept in a case at all times to protect them and protect their "zero." They should be zeroed at about 100 meters. I recommend the following sighting systems: Leupold, a laser range finder, Aquila, Schmidt and Bender, and Trijicon.

This is not a sniper manual—sniping is a separate, highly

specialized field within security. For security work, it is sufficient to be able to group up to 300 meters with an M4 equipped with an ACOG scope, but a 7.62 or heavier weapon is always better when available. The sniper team can follow a simple protocol: if no weapons are seen, fire a warning shot to the approaching vessel. However, your first priority is the safety of your crew. As always, your actions are dictated to a certain extent by circumstances, such as your location and other activity in the area. If guns are sighted, your shot should be to the outboard motor of their craft. If this elicits them to return fire, then you may shoot to kill. If the outboard is not visible, then a hull shot will work just the same. If no weapons are present and they continue to approach, then other weapons available to the maritime security team—including a sound gun, water cannon, or other nonlethal weapon—can be used. All are good, but none can compete with real firearms.

An alternative to a sniper system is a chain gun. A Negev is a 5.56mm belt-fed fully automatic weapon. It can be used to spray the water next to the pirate vessel, which does three things:

1. Shows them that you are serious and that you can and will kill them
2. Gives you a reference point from which to adjust your fire
3. Either entices them to shoot at you, which legally authorizes you to kill them, or scares them off

Pirates typically use hooks and ladders to scale the ship's high sides. To deter this, you can line the outside edges of your ship with razor wire. The wire deters the pirates altogether or slows them down. It also gives the security team a chance to use closer-range weapons, such as a 12-gauge Mossberg 590 A1 shotgun to suppress their will to mount.

Once a firefight breaks out with the crew of a pirate skiff, be prepared to be attacked with an RPG or automatic weapons. Your team needs to have two men running the sniper systems and one man spotting for them. The fourth man should be prepping the crew and ship for a battle and possible attempted boarding. The fourth man will put the crew into a safe room, which every ship should have. This room is heavily fortified and impenetrable, and has reinforced doors, its own air supply, bathrooms, water, food, Internet access, communications equipment, weapons, and, most important, the ability to override and control the entire ship. The safe room is of immense value when the crew is forced to seek refuge within it. Pirates have used saws and torches to crack open safe rooms and threaten the occupants with hand grenades and fire.

As with explosives and maritime sniping, marine security is a specialized field in the security business and needs specific expertise for its unique threats and limits.

BUS OR TRAIN TRAVEL

I recommend strongly against public bus or train travel. There are too many uncontrollable factors for the security team to deal with. Either mode of travel should be undertaken only as a last resort.

CHAPTER 25

Traveling in Groups

Protecting one man in a foreign environment is challenging and requires a dynamic and well-trained team, but protecting a group of people is exponentially more difficult. Of course, many of the principles used to protect one person are applicable to providing security to a group. Usually when securing a single individual, there are several guards and layers for that person, but when protecting a group you quickly lose that ratio. So, instead of four guards protecting one client, for example, you might have one guard protecting four clients. Those numbers aren't in your favor.

Some examples of when you might be engaged in providing group security are accompanying kids on a field trip, protecting foreign dignitaries on a trip abroad, and guarding a VIP family on vacation. Providing security for a group has several problems that you don't have when securing a fixed installation. Some might seem obvious, but they must be stated and understood in order to overcome them.

The locations you will be working in are foreign to you, when compared to your base location. Common base locations are a VIP's house or office and the consulate or courthouse you work out of daily. All the places the group of VIPs will go will be "new" to your staff and must be considered such for each trip, even if you have been there before. This is because the area traveled to isn't under your control, so you must remain sharp and ready, even more so than in the higher-profile areas. You must ask, "Was this trip publicized in the news?" "Is our route known to anyone else?" "Did someone put this on Facebook, telling the enemy exactly where and when we are going?" You need a battle plan before venturing into new territory with a group to protect.

Whether protecting a group or an individual, you rely on a few basic things: your security warrior skills and specific bodyguarding skills, your specific plan for that particular detail, and finally your fellow warriors.

There are always going to be unknown factors you can't plan for in advance because they are so unpredictable. You must have specific plans for general threats and rely on these to get you through the unpredictable occurrences. For example, you have an alternate driving route that can be used for several reasons (e.g., traffic, construction, earthquake, protest). It doesn't matter why you take the alternate. The fact is that you have an alternate route, and that's the plan for all road hazards and potential threats en route. Unknown factors always play a huge part in executive protection because of mobility and surrounding factors over which no one has control.

Whether protecting a VIP or a group of VIPs, it is best not to look like you're part of a security detail, so be low key. As stated earlier, an undercover operator has a huge advantage when dealing with the unknown factors you will face on the road, and especially when you're charged with protecting a number of people.

When working outside your facility, you don't have complete control over who enters or exits the structures. Often, the places you take your group to will be public spaces, such as restaurants, museums, or parks. These places aren't secure at all, so you must balance security concerns with the group members' freedom to enjoy their trip or outing. As always, you must do your best to spot suspicious parties or potentially dangerous situations long before they can endanger the security of your group.

Working proactively is the key to minimizing threats to groups.

For example, if there is a lawn service working outside the facility where you're going with your group, you must understand two things: (1) the workers aren't checked out by anyone on your security team, and (2) they have in their hands some very dangerous weapons, such as chain saws and machetes. Members of your group may have to pass by them, but do not allow them to get very close. You must watch the workers like a hawk through your sunglasses, remembering the scenarios you have played out in your mind how to best react to the particular threat they pose. Never show any prospective attackers your back. Your observation needs to be done inconspicuously. The bottom line is that every person is a threat and all objects can be weapons until proven otherwise.

New areas are new threat zones, such as the street or a mall. These threat zones must be protected from all possible angles. For example, when your party is walking down a street, it is important to have men on both sides of the street to scout the area in front of the group. From across the street you can see above the parties who are walking and above the rooftops and windows. This precaution is essential to see potential threats before it is too late. All areas your team enters should be considered unsecured until you have searched them.

For example, your group wants to eat at a restaurant, so the restaurant needs to be searched for suspicious parties in the parking lot, seating area, and bathrooms before the members of your party are permitted to enter. Plus, you must do this without disturbing the other patrons of the establishment. Every new structure you go into must be assessed on the appropriate level, and every person that nears you must be scrutinized. Of course, 99.98 percent of the time, things will go smoothly and be threat free, but you must be ready to strike at all times in order to do your job. And that job is to save the lives of the group members under your protection.

Remember, you're not creating a situation in which you're waiting to react—you're creating a situation in which you minimize the chances of your having to react. For example, you always sit in an establishment with your back to a wall and face the front door. Doing this minimizes your blind area and keeps your direction oriented to the area of greatest threat. The protected parties should avoid sitting next to windows when possible. Being next to a window makes them vulnerable from an attack originating outside, such as gunfire or a vehicle smashing through the window. Also, it makes it easier for a spy stationed outside to see where you're sitting, when you get up to go to the bathroom, or when you're leaving.

When reserving hotel rooms for VIPs, make sure you get rooms that are at the end of the hall of the third floor. The third floor is desirable because it doesn't take too long to leave the building in case of an emergency, such as a fire or bomb threat. The third floor is also high enough to prevent possible street-side penetration by climbers, stone throwers, or other threats. Being at the end of the hall lessens foot traffic and acts as a filter for anyone who attempts to get close to the protected rooms. Posting security staff outside the doors is easier if you have to deal with only one direction of potential travel. Security personnel should have the adjoining rooms to the ones where the VIPs are staying, on the side closer to the exit or elevator. This prevents eavesdropping and keeps staff close for immediate response if needed. Having an adjoining door is best if available. The curtains should remain drawn at all times, and movements must be kept secret from the hotel staff.

Essentially, you're in enemy territory the whole time you aren't in your own territory. In this case, enemy territory includes all areas not searched where people can enter without being checked. You simply don't have the strategic advantage, and the attacker will use the fact that this area can't be searched and checked thoroughly to his advantage. Avoid crowds, heavy traffic, dead ends, and being conspicuous so that you don't further disadvantage yourself and your group.

When protecting a large group, unique considerations must also be taken into account, including making each person in the group accountable, keeping them together, and moving them safely without unnecessarily inconveniencing their trip. There is an old saying that applies to security work: "Two is one and one is none." With that in mind, at a bare minimum you need to have two security warriors assigned to the detail to protect the group for both combat purposes and preventative and containment purposes. One reason for this necessity is that one of the men needs to act as an advance man, to go ahead of the VIPs to search the destination point and await the group. Scouting the location and searching it for suspicious activity, persons, or objects give the team a tremendous advantage and a heads-up on preventing catastrophe.

Of course, the scouting must be done undercover, or it will defeat the purpose. Once on location, the advance man will wait for the protected party to arrive and provide protection at the entrance, since we know that the group members are most vulnerable when transitioning from their automobiles to the intended destination. It is the forward intelligence agent who gives the incoming group the final OK to enter the parking lot of a restaurant, park, or any other location, because he has driven and rehearsed the route and scenarios beforehand. Once the forward intelligence agent is certain that there are no visible threats, the group members can come in (preferably through a back entrance) with the second security force, which is in the vehicle. The driver pulls as close to the entrance as possible and leaves the motor running the whole time the party is disembarking. The designated warrior will exit, opening the fresh space, and the protected party members will transition smoothly to the given location, where the second warrior waits inside.

In an ideal situation, the forward intelligence personnel will go to a new location, city, venue, restaurant, or wherever, days in advance to scout and assess. Even if the destination is a park or building that you have visited previously, you must still assess the threats and build your battle plan for this specific trip. Knowing is half the battle, but this isn't always feasible. You must arrive with at least enough time to search the facility and surrounding areas. Often, you will have to rely on maps to provide information that the on-site survey would have yielded if it had been done. All your battle plans and contingency plans, routes, and other pieces of intelligence must be built around the maps of the location in which you're working.

The security team should provide the protected members of the group with umbrellas rain or shine. The umbrella isn't for protection against sun or rain; it is for protection against the greatest threat to the team—snipers. When exiting the vehicle, the umbrellas provide concealment from a sniper's aim. A mobile tent might be better in certain group scenarios, but it is more trouble to use and it requires a static location. The forward intelligence team will have to assess sniper vulnerability based on location and other factors and decide what countermeasures should be taken. Remember, if an attack happens, drop the umbrellas and move the group quickly to the safety and mobility of the vehicles or the interior of the structure (whichever is closer).

The vehicle (or vehicles if more than one is needed for your group) is reverse-parked as close as possible to the exit of the structure. The engine is left running, and the driver remains behind the wheel at all times. The driver must prevent anyone from blocking him, including delivery trucks or standing cars. One or two warriors will enter with the group members, while another waits outside the facility watching anyone who enters or exits the parking lot and building.

Each team should be assembled according to the size of the group—the more people in the group, the more security staff is needed. As a general principle, the warriors aren't switched throughout the workday or the work assignment; each security team should be one organic group from the planning stages to the end of the last day of the trip. This is maintained for consistency, battle preparedness, and secrecy purposes. The group trip must be as compartmentalized and contained as possible. Unlike when protecting a static facility, there is no change of guard until the trip is over.

A specific timetable must be determined before the trip begins, specifying the destination, the time it takes to get there, the length of the stay, and the departure time. The locations, routes, and times should be incorporated into this plan and agreed on by all the members of the team. All reservations are made in a fake name or in the name of a bodyguard to avoid exposing the location and time of the group's arrival.

Before undertaking a group assignment, you need to think about how many people you will be responsible for protecting and how many men and how much equipment it will take to realistically provide that level of protection. In some cases, you may have to make do with what you have as far as staff and equipment go; in other situations, you will have ample men and equipment to run the detail completely and securely.

Logistics for a large group can be a nightmare, but you can't allow them to become a distraction or derail the trip. One way to do this is to make sure that details are taken care of during the planning phase. Examples of some things that can be planned in advance are food, tour guide services, drivers, vehicle maintenance, and accommodations. Each logistical element must be personally reviewed by the team and approved before departure.

As when traveling with a single VIP, security personnel must memorize all the preferred and alternate routes for the group before the trip, as well as what signs must be present to justify detouring to an alternate route. Also, safe havens, police stations, and medical facilities are identified along the route in advance. This is especially critical when traveling with a group since your odds of needing emergency services rise as the number of people in your party increases.

CHAPTER 26

Security During Meals

If the eating establishment structure is small, such as a café, scan the inside and then wait outside for your client or clients to finish. Try to blend in; don't look the part when you're undercover. Be alert but sit down. Check the inside, but do it as you make your way to the bathroom. If you want to get a feel for a customer or other bystander, engage him in brief, casual conversation and get a feel for his response. Intuition is important, so use it and trust it in this situation.

When on the move with a VIP or a group, warriors must fuel up as well. If a two-man team is being used, one man will eat while the other stands guard, and then they will switch. You should eat healthy fast food, such as sandwiches, fruit, yogurt, and other quick fixes. Don't drink alcohol while on duty, and don't eat foods that may not agree with you or take a long time to digest. You don't need the distraction. Don't go into restaurants where it takes you a long time to order, prepare, eat, and pay for your food. In a seated restaurant, you abdicate too much control to the wait staff; you need to remain in control as much as possible.

After everyone has eaten and the bill has been paid, you leave the structure first to scan the area; only after it is deemed safe will the VIP exit to his transportation.

CONCLUSION

As discussed, security work is tougher than being a soldier or a police officer. Your work is reactionary and requires you to always be alert and ready to act. You're not responding to an incident that has taken place, like a policeman would. You're at the incident when it takes place and the subject of the attack. You're not on the attack, like a team of soldiers conducting a raid; you're fighting from the disadvantage of having to play catch-up and react to the stimulus. You don't choose the time, location, or method of the fight, yet you must be ready for all possibilities.

The most challenging obstacle to overcome in security work is that of boredom, and the complacency that accompanies it. You will struggle with being on constant alert for months at a time without incident. You will do your best to remain sharp and focused, and keep your skills honed for that once-in-a-lifetime challenge to do your job well enough to save lives and defeat the enemy. A trick I use to fight complacency is to try to find the one suspicious person in each assignment or detail. There will always be one. Trying to find that one person and running mental scenarios will keep you on your toes, and you can think of it as a game to counter boredom.

I hope that this book will help you prepare for a career as a security warrior. It contains the lessons, knowledge, and skills that I have picked up throughout my career. They have kept my clients and my team safe in some pretty hostile areas. Good luck and stay safe.

ABOUT THE AUTHOR

Garret Machine was born in Miami, Florida, to American-born parents. He graduated from Valley Forge Military Academy in Wayne, Pennsylvania, and then attended Florida International University. After graduation in 2002 Machine went to Israel to join the Israel Defense Forces (IDF).

Machine served warrior, medic, and firearms tactics instructor in an IDF undercover unit for several years. This unit specialized in undercover work, urban warfare, targeted assassinations, and kidnapping of wanted militants throughout the West Bank. After participating in close to 100 missions with his unit, Machine went to the Interdisciplinary Center in Hertzlia, Israel, where he earned a master's degree in homeland security and counterterrorism.

Following his military service, Machine worked as a field bodyguard for the Israeli Ministry of Defense. Unlike traditional bodyguard or executive protection details, he was part of a unit that worked exclusively in the West Bank in high-risk areas. A typical detail was in small teams using off-road and armored trucks, where he was equipped with an M4 rifle, pistol, and 7.62mm armored vest. After this, Machine joined the ranks of the Israeli National Police Force, where he served until 2010.

Shortly after completing his service to Israel, Machine moved to the United States, where he now provides security consultations. Other credentials include:

- IDF firearms instructor
- Georgia State POST firearms instructor
- Pennsylvania State Police lethal weapons training instructor
- NRA law enforcement instructor
- Licensed State of Florida firearms and armed security instructor
- Recently featured on Discovery Channel's *One Man Army*

You can reach Machine at Garretmachine@yahoo.com.